T0195581

It Starts with Me

Feel Good within and Become Your Happiest, Healthiest Self

YVETTE LE BLOWITZ

BALBOA.
PRESS

A DIVISION OF HAY HOUSE

Balboa Press books may be ordered through booksellers or by contacting:

Balboa Press
A Division of Hay House
1663 Liberty Drive
Bloomington, IN 47403
www.balboapress.com
1 (877) 407-4847

Because of the dynamic nature of the Internet, any web addresses or
links contained in this book may have changed since publication and
may no longer be valid. The views expressed in this work are solely those
of the author and do not necessarily reflect the views of the publisher,
and the publisher hereby disclaims any responsibility for them.

The author of this book does not dispense medical advice or prescribe the use
of any technique as a form of treatment for physical, emotional, or medical
problems without the advice of a physician, either directly or indirectly. The
intent of the author is only to offer information of a general nature to help
you in your quest for emotional and spiritual well-being. In the event you use
any of the information in this book for yourself, which is your constitutional
right, the author and the publisher assume no responsibility for your actions.

Any people depicted in stock imagery provided by Thinkstock are
models, and such images are being used for illustrative purposes only.
Certain stock imagery © Thinkstock.

Print information available on the last page.

ISBN: 978-1-5043-0965-3 (sc)
ISBN: 978-1-5043-0968-4 (e)

Balboa Press rev. date: 08/01/2017

CONTENTS

Twenty-one-Day Wellness Guide to Your
Happiest, Healthiest, Spiritual Self 85

ACKNOWLEDGMENTS

To my family, friends, Spa It Girl blog readers, followers, and anyone who has ever supported me: thank you. I am truly grateful for all of your love, light, and positive support.

And to my brand-new reader who has just picked up my book, *It Starts with Me*: thanks for choosing to become your happiest and healthiest self.

For my mum, who taught me to believe in myself and to never give up on my dream. I am truly blessed and love you so much. You are so kind, loving, caring, beautiful inside and out, and a true inspiration.

I love you from the bottom of my heart and soul, more than you will ever know. Thanks for always being there for me no matter what. When I think about my life and the person I have become, I am so grateful to call you my mum.

You taught me how to be kind and caring towards others, and now because of you, I love to give more than I get.

I will always remember the good times we shared together, and especially the amazing family holidays we went on each year.

Thank you for buying me a book every single Friday when I was a kid, and for writing in the front of the book your heartfelt message of "To Yvette. Love, Mum."

You truly started my love for storytelling, reading, and books, and it has been an absolute blessing. Thank you.

I am so happy that I now personally sign a copy of my very first self-help book and write my own message in it for you. What a dream come true. Thank you!

Love you always,
Yvette

INTRODUCTION

"I believe everything starts from within."

I wrote this book so you could become your happiest, healthiest self. You deserve to feel good within, and I am so happy to be able to share with you my very own go-to wellness lifestyle tips that don't cost the earth.

In this book, you are taken on a twenty-one-day journey so you can become your happiest and healthiest self. I invite you to make the time each day to focus your attention inwards, to connect with your true inner self, and to take care of and love yourself no matter what.

You deserve to be happy and healthy to live your own authentic dreams, and I am going to show you how.

My Go-to Wellness Tips and Rituals

Here are my go-to wellness lifestyle tips that I wanted to share, so you can become your happiest, healthiest self.

Be Present

Each day when you wake up, connect with yourself first before anyone else. Focus inwards and on your breath. Lie or sit in your bed and simply be. Feel the rise and fall of your chest, listen to your breath, and become aware. Have a little stretch while in bed, and take the time to become fully present and connected with yourself before grabbing your mobile phone and looking at what everyone else is doing on social media.

It's so important to connect with the self first before anyone else, especially at the start of each day. This simple daily practice will help you connect from within; it will allow you to start your day with ease and in a nice, gentle, spiritual way. It will help you become connected within and fully present before you jump out of bed to start your day.

Practice Daily Meditation

Connect to your breath and simply be.

Taking up meditation has seriously changed my life. It has allowed me to become my happiest and healthiest self, and this has happened all by simply focussing my attention inwards and on my own breath.

I truly believe mediation has contributed to me, creating the life I want and living my dreams. Everything changed for the better as soon as I started meditating regularly. Meditation transformed my life, and because of that, naturally I want to share this powerful practice with you so you can also feel calm and at peace within.

If you have never meditated before, that's okay. It's easier than you think. All you need to do is find a nice, comfortable place and space. You can either sit up or lie down. Close your eyes and simply focus your attention inwards and on your breath.

Take a few big, deep breaths in through your nose and out through your mouth. Simply let everything go and relax. Once you have settled and feel grounded, take a big, deep breath in through your nose for the count of two and out through your mouth for the count of four.

You can make your inhales and exhales to suit your own natural rhythm and count. There is no such thing as the right way or the wrong way when it comes to meditating; it's all about focussing on your own breath and becoming present and connected.

If find your mind wandering, that's okay. Simply guide your attention back inwards and onto your breath.

When I first started meditating, I thought I couldn't do it because I had thoughts rising and falling during my meditation practice. I originally thought I had to have a clear mind, with not one thought coming up.

I later found out that when you meditate, it's natural for thoughts to occur within. Every time I found myself getting caught up in the thought, I had to focus back inwards on my breath, become the observer, and let the thoughts rise and fall with no judgement at all.

There are so many guided meditations out there, and also online for free through YouTube. I originally started out meditating by using guided meditations online through YouTube, and then I started doing guided meditations at the end of my yoga classes.

I found when I was starting out meditating, having someone else guide me was excellent because it helped keep me focus on what I needed to do. I was unsure at the time what to do, and I wondered if I was doing it right or wrong. I later discovered there is no right or wrong way; it's all about focussing on your own breath.

Now I am able to meditate on my own anywhere or anytime, without any music, apps, or guided meditations on YouTube. I love meditation so much that I even hold my own guided meditation classes so that others can feel peace, love, and light from within. Through Spa it Girl (www.spaitgirl.com), I have been getting so many people into meditating. I have loved seeing the transformations of those who decide to give it a go: they see their whole lives turn around and change for the better, becoming their happiest, healthiest, confident selves. They start living their dreams, and it is so amazing that it makes me more inspired to share meditation with more and more people globally.

When it comes to picking what guided meditation you should do, the best thing is to focus your attention inwards and to connect with how you are feeling. Some days you might need a guided meditation for stress, anxiety, sleep, or relaxation.

When you take a moment to be quiet and check in with how you are truly feeling from within, your inner self will guide you to what type of guided meditation practice you need.

All of the answers to your questions come from within. You simply have to take the time to be quiet and sit in silence.

Do you need to meditate for stress? Heartbreak? Depression? Anxiety? Study? Self-love and acceptance? Positivity? What is it you need? Take a moment to become silent and present, and your inner self will guide you.

The mind is constantly multitasking, and at times it might feel like it never stops and can always be on the go, even if you are sitting down. Cultivating a daily meditation will help you feel calm and peace from within; it will help you switch off relax and bring down your stress levels.

Meditation will assist with overcome anything. You will go from doing to simply being.

Meditation is the perfect stress reliever, and if you start practicing meditation during the good times, then when the bad times hit when you least expected, you have the best stress management practice to see you through.

When you meditate, it's like going on a mini holiday but without the cost. The more you do it, the more benefits it brings in all aspects of your life.

Daily meditation is essential for your health and wellness. It's a must-do—it's as simple as that.

Do your best to meditate daily, even if you start out practicing meditation for a few minutes. It's not about how many minutes or for how long; it's about focusing on your breath and becoming fully present. Depending on how you are feeling, some days fifteen minutes of mediation won't feel like enough, and you might need to meditate for even longer when you tune in to how you are feeling. Your inner self will guide you.

When you meditate, you will find your peace and experience a calm state of being. It will allow you to feel a happier, healthier, more positive, and more loving self, being connected from within. Meditation will make you feel whole again.

Along my spiritual journey, I have tried so many different types of meditations: chanting meditations, kundalini meditations, guided meditations, meditation apps, meditation DVDs, and guided meditations on YouTube. I am always open to trying new types of meditation practices that are out there, and I invite you to do the same. I still have so many meditations to try but that really excites me. When you start to meditate daily and feel the health and wellness benefits that come with it, meditation becomes a joy and not a chore.

Make mediation part of your life. I truly believe that meditation is key and an essential day-to-day wellness practice that will help anyone living in these crazy, busy times.

If you want to feel less stressed and overwhelmed, and you want to be happier, healthier, relaxed, calm, and at peace within, then meditate. It will help you feel healthy and well in so many ways.

Even though some days I might only spend five or fifteen minutes meditating, what I get back in health, wellness, happiness far outweighs the time I spend meditating that day. That's how powerful meditating truly is.

What do you do if you know that meditation is good for you, but you still have that conversation in your head that you don't have time to fit it in because you are too busy? You change the story from within with my meditation mantra: "If I have time to brush my teeth and check my social media news feed, then I have time to meditate. I can meditate, and I will meditate."

By saying this meditation mantra to yourself over and over, you are changing your story from within and are reaffirming that you do have time and will make time, because meditation is part of your day-to-day life.

It takes a bit of work, and I am not going to pretend that you will say the mantra a couple of times and turn into a meditation Zen master. However, by changing the story from within, it will allow you to create space within and realise that if you have time to brush your teeth or check your social media news feed, then you do have time to meditate. To make it even easier, after you brush your teeth or check your social media, tag on your meditation practice straight after that. That will build it into your daily habit.

If the whole meditation mantra doesn't work for you, then try building meditation into your day with your other routines. If you have to catch the train every day for work, use that time whilst sitting down in the train. Close your eyes and put in your earphones. Simply focus on your breath and try listening to beautiful, soothing music or a guided meditation.

If you have lunch in the park, then use your lunch break to do a nice, easy, gentle meditation practice. It will help with your stress levels and make you feel calm and at peace.

Make time to create space within. Once you start meditating and discover the health and wellness benefit it brings, you will start to see your life changing in every positive way. You will appreciate just how amazing this simple daily practice ritual is, and you will probably wonder why you haven't been doing it for years. I know, because I once asked the same question.

Meditation is a daily must-do, just like brushing your teeth or checking your social media. If you want to live your happiest, healthiest spiritual life and change the way you feel from within, mediation is key. If you want to live the life of your dreams, then meditation is a must.

Wake Up and Set Your Intentions

She created the life she wanted, even when others said no to her ideas and dreams.

If you want to manifest the life you want and live your dreams, than you have to wake up and set your intentions. If you want to lose weight, then write it down and get clear what your intention is. Make it clear how you are going to make your intention become your reality.

If you want to lose weight, you have to say it and define it. Do you want to lose weight to feel good or to look good? Or is it because the doctor has told you that you don't have a choice because you health is at risk? In order to know where you're going, you have to know why you are going.

Write down what you intend to do each day so you can start working towards your own personal goals. Every day, wake up and set your intention. Write down what action you are going to take. You are bringing yourself closer to making your intention your reality.

When I was on my weight-loss journey, I would wake up every morning and set my intention. I would make it crystal clear what action I was going to take to make my goals happen. I would write down things like, "Today I am going for a twenty-minute walk so I can feel good within."

By waking up and setting my intention, I then make it happen. Day after day, I was slowly co-creating along with my inner spirit and the power of the universe, making my intention become my reality. Eventually I reached my weight-loss goal and lost over twenty-five kilos naturally, all from waking up each day and setting my intention and then taking action to make it happen. Every day I did my best to follow through on what I set out to do.

I still wake up and set my intentions each day, but my intentions are now totally different than when I was working towards my own personal weight-loss goals. Setting your intentions is a very personal thing, and no one can set your intentions for you or make things happen. Everything you manifest or create starts from within.

Get clear on what you want and why, set your intention, and make it happen. Aim to do one thing every single waking day that will bring you closer to your own personal goals, and before you know it, you will be creating and living the life you want.

Setting your daily intentions is so powerful; I wouldn't be where I am today without it. Create the like you want, wake up each day, and set your intentions.

Exercise

Exercise makes everything feel right.

Exercise makes me feel good. I have always loved the way exercise has made me feel, and I find every time exercise, I feel great after it.

I learnt from a very young age that it didn't matter if I had money or not. Everyone could feel good through exercising, and no amount of money in the world could ever make me the fastest or best runner in the field.

As a kid, I loved to walk, run, ride my bike, play tennis, play netball, dance, play school sports, run long distance, and do cross country. I discovered it didn't matter what type of sports I tried; it all made me feel good.

I later went on and become an aerobics teacher and a fitness and personal trainer. That's how much I loved exercise and helping others to exercise so they could also feel inspired, motivated, happy, and good from within.

When we are kids, it was much easier because we had all the time and energy in the world. When we become adults, life can become crazy busy, and we might feel we don't have enough time, energy, or motivation.

I truly believe in this day and age that exercise is the key for feeling good and getting through the good times and the bad times. When you exercise, it makes everything feel right.

To create a regular exercise practice, you need to find a way to move that makes you feel good and that you truly love. If you love to dance, then dance. If you love to walk, then walk. If you love to swim, then swim. What is it you love? When you take a moment to sit in silence and ask the question, your inner spirit will guide you. Exercise is scientifically proven to give release feel-good endorphins, so it's the best way to feel good within and to lift your mood.

When you live an active life, it will do wonders for your health, wellness, happiness, skin, and relationships. It will also help you create and live the life you truly want.

Exercise can take you from having no friends and feeling lonely and isolated, to having loads of friends and never feeling lonely or isolated. Exercise is such a social thing that it helps you feel reconnected with those you love and your community.

You can stay motivated to exercise by catching up with a friend to go for a walk or run. Try a group fitness class at your local gym, a yoga class at a studio, or a personal trainer appointment. Sign up for a boot camp or any empowering workout challenges. There are so many ways to stay motivated when you start looking at all of the different options where you live. You can now access online workout classes through YouTube, websites, and apps. There are so many fitness inspirations online to help inspire and motivate you.

It's important to mix up your workout routines so you can get results and don't get bored. Boredom can lead to not feeling motivated to exercise at all. Try new types of exercise and workouts, mix things up, step outside of your comfort zone, and challenge yourself. You will learn so much about yourself by doing so, and it will also make exercising really fun and interesting.

Aim to exercise at least three times a week for thirty minutes. Choose to move in a way that makes you feel good. Add some resistance training if you are not a fan of lifting weights in the gym or doing a full, high-intensity interval training (HIIT).

Work on your strength through practicing yoga. I have found practicing yoga and having to lift my own weight is more enjoyable than lifting weighting weights at the gym. However, we are different, and everything comes back to doing what you love and what is right for you.

My sister loves going to the gym, doing a gym session using the cardio machines, and then doing her resistance training using the weights in the weight room. Even though we are sisters, we have a different love for resistance training, and that is perfectly fine.

It's important that when you workout, it's for you and no one else. Do what you love and what makes you feel good. By doing this, you will want to come back and exercise more and more. It will become part of your life.

If you are trying to lose weight, it's always great to mix up your workouts so that your body, mind, and spirit don't get used to the same old, same old.

It can be really frustrating if you are putting the effort in and turning up to work out, but you're not seeing any results. When you mix it up, your body is challenged; different muscle groups are being worked. Then the results happen.

When it comes to my yoga practice, I never practice the same class twice. Every time I practice yoga, it's a totally different yoga class and flow. I am always challenging myself and learning more about my body, mind, and spirit every time.

Even when it comes to my love for walking, I mix it up as much as I can. One day I might walk up a hill and do 1,400 stairs. The next time, it might be a gradual incline walk, then a flat power walk, then interval training with walking and jogging. I am continually mixing it up.

I exercise to feel good, and it has nothing to do with body image. When you exercise to feel good instead of saying, "I must exercise to lose a certain weight," it takes all of the pressure and stress out of it, and it becomes more enjoyable. Life should be enjoyed, so make your exercise about feeling good, and enjoy it!

I also try to make every workout count, and I do my best to put as much effort in when working out.

If I choose to exercise and do a walk, then I am only going do my best to give it my all. I listen to my favourite music to help motivate and inspire me. I work up a sweat, and at the end when it is all over, I have set my own personal best and can have a drink, a rest. That's when my own natural, feel-good endorphins start kicking in, and I am personally rewarded from within.

As a kid, I used to jog all the time. I loved long-distance running and would always set new personal bests. My personal best for a ten-kilometre run is forty-three minutes and five seconds. Some weeks I used to run up to fifty kilometres, and I loved getting lost in music and running. It helped to take my mind off everything.

Over time, however, from pounding the pavement to teaching countless high-impact aerobics to doing loads of tuck jumps, I started getting injuries. There came a point when I could only walk fifteen minutes on a flat surface, and my knee would feel like it was on fire. I was advised that I needed to do low-impact sports like walking and yoga. I went from a runner to having to become a walker.

At first it was hard to accept that what I could do in my twenties was different to my late thirties. However, I accepted that with age comes change, and I had to adapt. I started to appreciate what my body could physically do now, and I was grateful that I was still able to exercise. I needed to start living in the now.

I learnt to become grateful for the types of exercise I could do, and now I love walking and yoga. I no longer yearn to be my twenty-year-old self. I choose to live in the now.

When you appreciate how fortunate you are able to move and exercise, you create a healthy relationship within. You discover that being able to exercise is truly a gift and that no amount of money could ever give you the amount of feel-good, happy, healthy endorphins that exercise brings.

If you want to become your best version and live the life of your dreams, being active is key. It's a must-do to feel good within. Work on making exercise part of your life. Don't focus on how hard it is focus on how good it makes you feel. Connect to the feeling and choose to exercise for self-love and not self-hate.

When I was twenty-five kilos heavier, even sitting on the ground to put on my walking shoes was a workout in itself! I struggled at times to tie my own shoelaces. I had put loads of extra weight on because so many things in my life went pear-shaped around the same time. I went from being really fit to unfit, so when I made a comeback, I had to start all over again. I had to regain my fitness, strength, happiness, health, and confidence.

I started my weight-loss journey by walking ten to fifteen minutes. That was my workout and all I could manage to do at the start. However, by continually showing up, I eventually got fitter, and my walks got longer. At places that I once had to stop at to catch my breath, I would walk by with a big smile.

Being active and exercising is always going to be a work in progress, and there is no limit when it comes to getting fit.

Exercise and getting fit looks different to each of us, so it's important to find away to move that is right for you. Create your own moves and rules. Exercise is a lifelong journey, and you will always be learning and evolving as an individual. Go with the flow and adapt to age and lifestyle changes.

Life is full of ups and downs, and some weeks you will be flat out and only get to do a couple of workouts. Then there will be other weeks when you might manage to get in five workouts.

Go with the flow, accept, and adapt to change. Don't beat yourself up. Simply accept life as it unfolds, and do your best to work out when you feel like it. Listen to your body and your own inner needs.

Don't put yourself under a strict exercise routine. Instead, exercise with ease. This approach to exercise will make it much easier to stick to it, and it's a more enjoyable.

There are going to be times in your life that for whatever reason, you might not be able to exercise because you have fallen ill, get an injury, or are working twelve-hour days. Whatever the reason, remember that you always have the ability to start over again. You can work to become happier, healthier, and fitter within, all through creating a brand-new exercise routine.

Never beat yourself up or think that you have let yourself go. Sometimes things happen that are out of our control, and when you are in the middle of a crisis, your exercise routine can come to a grinding halt.

Life is not always smooth sailing and is going to knock you down at times. When it does, do your best to bounce back. Use exercise to feel good within and to make everything feel right.

You have the power to change the way you feel from within, and exercise is key.

Smile

Smile and light up your own world and the whole world.

I love to smile every single day. I couldn't live without it. It makes me feel so good inside. I smile to be kind. I smile to make others feel good. I even smile at others whilst on public transport or in a line-up waiting to be served.

When you smile, it will make you feel good. No matter what type of day you are having, simply smile. I think smiling is the easiest way to connect to your inner self, the universe, and everyone else.

When you smile, it radiates your love, light, and positivity. That energy attracts so much more than if you didn't smile at all.

Nourish Yourself from the Inside Out

Nourish yourself with fresh, healthy, plant-based, and unprocessed foods so you can feel good.

Nourish yourself each day so that you can feel good from the inside out. Do your best to eat healthy, fresh fruits and vegetables and unprocessed foods. It is recommended that for adults, we eat at least five servings of vegetables and two servings of fruit every day.

I try to keep my healthy living simple, and I do my best to eat as much natural, plant-based, fresh foods as I can. I choose to eat a variety of fruit and vegetables that are like the colours of the rainbow. What does that mean? It means I choose different coloured fruit and vegetables, like green foods (green apples, spinach, broccoli), orange foods (carrots, pumpkin, oranges), red foods (raspberries and strawberries), and purple and blue foods (passion fruit, blueberries).

The different coloured fruits and vegetables have different vitamins and minerals to offer. Aim to make your plate or bowl have a colour from each of the groups. It not only looks pretty but tastes fresh and delicious.

Eating like a rainbow is how I refer to it, and that is how I go about selecting the different coloured fruits and vegetables.

22

I personally love knowing where my food comes from, who grew it, and who created it. When I make my own healthy food, I know what ingredients I am putting in and what is going into it. When it comes to making my favourite protein balls, I love how I can make ten protein balls for the price of one pre-made protein ball from a store. It's a great feeling to create your own healthy, nourishing food, and it's rewarding too. I find making my own food is a great way to switch off. It allows me to become present because I am so focussed on what I am doing that I let go of what went on before, or what might go on in the future. It brings me right back to the now.

If you want to feel good within, eat fresh, plant-based fruits and vegetables and other healthy, natural ingredients. I have found the more plant-based foods I add to my day-to-day life, the better I feel.

The more food you can eat that has been grown from Mother Earth the better. Organic produce is always best because it has fewer chemicals. I know this might not be possible for everyone, so if you can pick up locally grown, seasonal produce and natural ingredients from your local farmers' market, that is a great way.

When it comes to healthy eating, adding in carbohydrates that are grain-based foods like breads, oats, muesli, rice, and quinoa is great. However you can get carbohydrates from fruits, vegetables, legumes, and low-fat dairy foods.

Carbohydrates contain essential vitamins and minerals. Despite some of the different weight-loss fads out there that encourage people to have a low-carb diet in order to lose weight, having carbohydrates provides us with the most essential nutrient, glucose, which is the preferred source of energy for our brains and muscles. We need glucose for survival.

Protein is essential for the growth, maintenance, and repair of body cells. You can obtain protein from animal foods like poultry, fish, milk, and eggs, or from plant-based foods like beans, peas, and lentils. These day's everyone has different needs, so it's about finding a source of protein that you personally love. Including protein into your meals will help satisfy your hunger and prevent you from unhealthy snacking.

Fats are another important thing to have when it comes to healthy eating. Fats help cushion our organs and contribute to our cell growth and development. They also allow us to absorb essential vitamins like A, D, E, and K. Eating good fats that come from vegetables, nuts, seeds, and fish are called monounsaturated and polyunsaturated fats, and they help by reducing bad cholesterol, reducing heart disease and stroke, and keeping healthy the brain and joints.

My go-to healthy fat is avocado. I love it so much that I always have one on my kitchen bench, ready to be eaten. I add avocado to pretty much everything, from my salads to toast. Avocado is also a source of fibre, and when people ask me for my skincare tips, I always credit avocados because I have personally seen a real difference since eating them.

Another thing we all need is fibre. Fibre has a cleansing effect, and it helps with food moving through the digestive system. When you consume fibre regularly, it can help promote the growth of good bacteria, and that is essential for maintaining our overall health and well-being—and of course being regular. Fibre also helps us feel full between meals and helps us from overeating or unhealthy snacking.

When it comes to healthy eating, do your best with everything in moderation. If you still find you are at a loose end and what you are eating isn't satisfying your own personal needs, then make the time to speak to a professional nutritionist or dietician, who will be able to help, knowing what amounts of nutrients, vitamins, and types of foods and servings you should be eating. Everything will be tailored for you because it can get so confusing, and there is so much information out there about what food you should or shouldn't eat. I think it's best to speak to a medical professional if you have tried everything and are still not feeling your best, because food is our life source and force; it's what gives us our daily energy, and it can either make us feel great or like crap. It's important that we are doing our best to nourish ourselves from the inside out.

Every country has its own food servings recommendations, but as a guide, the National Health and Medical Research Council (NHMRC) of Australia suggests the following.

- Eat plenty of vegetables, legumes. and fruits
- Eat plenty of cereals (including breads, rice, pasta, and noodles), preferably wholegrain
- Include lean meat, fish, poultry, and/or alternatives
- Include milks, yoghurts, cheeses, and/or alternatives. Reduced-fat varieties should be chosen where possible
- Drink plenty of water

And take care to:

- Limit saturated fat and moderate total fat intake
- Choose foods low in salt
- Limit your alcohol intake if you choose to drink
- Consume only moderate amounts of sugars and foods containing added sugars.

When I was on my own personal weight-loss journey, a couple of things I did was cut out my sugar in all of my cups of tea and coffee. I simply went cold turkey. I was having two teaspoons of sugar in everything, and when I sat back one day and worked out how much sugar I was adding to my day, it blew me away.

I grew up as a kid with my father working at the local sugar mill. He used to look after the machinery that made it. Naturally, I loved sugar as a kid, and while growing up I had sugar on everything. I couldn't get enough sugar and loved it so much.

Not having any sugar at all was a little weird and a real challenge, but I made it easier for myself by not having any sugar in the house. I completely got rid of it. By simply not having sugar in my house, I got used to having no sugar. Eventually, when people asked me if I wanted sugar, I would say no.

I found that cutting out adding sugar to everything made a real difference. What works for me might not work for you, and it's all about finding what works for you and trying lots of little lifestyle shifts.

I don't even have sugar in my cupboard, but more recently when I had family staying with me, I remembered that most people love having sugar in their cups of tea or coffee. I now have those sugar satchels in my cupboard, and I make sure to support my sugar cane–farming hometown. I always support locally made Australian sugar whenever I can.

Another lifestyle change I made along my own weight-loss journey was cutting out drinking alcohol. I went from a wine drinker to a water drinker, and I have to say it's been the best thing I ever did.

Cutting out drinking alcohol definitely changed the way I felt inside. It helped me lose that unwanted weight, and it made everything seem right. I became healthier and happier, and I was clearly able to set my goals and work towards my goals like never before.

Not waking up and feeling sick on the weekend is the greatest gift that I could possibly give to myself. Every now and again when I am on a Spa It Girl luxury spa media trip, I might enjoy a nice glass or two of a luxury champagne thanks to my beautiful host. However, alcohol is no longer part of my daily lifestyle, and I have to say it's the best I have ever felt.

It took me quite a while to work this out, because in Australia drinking is very much part of the culture. However, knowing what I know now, I truly believe if you want to feel good within, then cutting out alcohol is key, or at least taking the approach of everything in moderation.

Even in my thirties, I received a lot of peer pressure for choosing not to drink. However, as an older and wiser soul,

I was able to handle it and was able to put my own health and wellness first. I was not as easily influenced anymore.

I tend to now look at consumable products that cost money with a very different approach. I also ask a question: "If I am going to consume this product, is it going to make me feel good, or make me sick?" When I look at consumable products like that, it makes choosing healthy things so much easier.

I love to know where my food has come from, who made it, and who created it. I am always grateful for the amazing work farmers do, because they bring us fresh food and our life energy source, which allows us to live a healthy, happy life. I am grateful for all of their hard work and never take it for granted. Being grateful for the food you are eat will help build a healthy relationship with not only the food but those who have created it for you.

When you eat, do your best to eat mindfully. Take your time when you eat. Slow down and chew your food. Don't rush it. It can take a little bit of practice to slow down and chew our food properly because we are always so busy, but it will help with not overeating and making ourselves feel sick.

It is believed that it can take up to twenty minutes for your body and brain to connect, and for your mind to realise you are full. Take your time while eating, and practice mindfulness while eating. Become fully present and aware of what you are eating, chew your food, and take it slowly.

Eating mindfully means becoming aware of the food that has been prepared and is right in front of you. Take the time to see what it looks like, smells like, and tastes like. Connect and become present whilst eating; your digestive system will thank you for it.

When you make food for yourself or those you love, make it from your heart and soul. Create healthy, fresh meals to nourish your body, mind, and soul. Soul food that is made from your heart and soul, or someone else's, always tastes better than any food that you get out of a packet or that has come from a factory.

When I was overweight, I didn't turn to any fad diets or expensive weight-loss products. Instead, I chose to eat natural, plant-based foods from Mother Earth and as much unprocessed foods as I could. By eating healthy fresh food and ingredients, I lost the twenty-five kilos in a natural way that didn't cost me a lot.

No matter what food addictions you have or the obstacles you have to overcome, do your best and nourish yourself from within with fresh, healthy, unprocessed foods and ingredients.

I have personally had my own struggle with food addictions and being a comfort eater. I use to use food as my emotional escape, and I would turn to food to comfort me. As an emotional eater I would turn to chocolate—and not just a small bite. I would eat a family-sized chocolate block. Eating this always gave me comfort and instantly picked up my mood.

I experienced the sugar highs and lows, and after I ate so much chocolate that it would make me feel sick, the guilt would kick in. Why did I eat so much chocolate? Emotionally, it didn't fix anything—it simply contributed to putting on extra, unwanted kilos.

I overcame my emotional eating by managing my stress through meditation, along with choosing fresh, healthy, unprocessed foods and ingredients. Ever since I started meditation and nourishing myself from the inside out, I no longer struggle with being an emotional eater or having food addictions.

Get Your Beauty Sleep

We all need our beauty sleep. It's a must!

Sleep is a must-have if you want to become your happiest and healthiest self. The recommendation is eight hours of sleep per night. When you are asleep, it allows time for your brain to repair and rest your cells, body, mind, and spirit. In order to live a healthy and active life, you need to wake up feeling like you had a good night's sleep.

Create a routine bedtime pattern and count backwards eight hours from the time you have to get up. Lay off the coffee after noon, because research has found that a cup of coffee can take between six to twelve hours to wear off. If you are not able to fall asleep at night and are wondering why, it could be that you had a cup of coffee in the afternoon, and it still hasn't worn off.

If you feel wide awake and alert, chances are the caffeine is in your system. Or perhaps you have a lot of things on your mind; if that is the case, get your notepad out and pen, and start journaling. This will help with clearing your mind.

Try drinking herbal tea in the afternoon. If you need a caffeine fix, switch to black tea. You will still get a little pick-me-up but with more relaxing benefits, and it will help you sleep better.

Try to go back to old-school habits like not contacting anyone after 9:00 p.m. That's also a great away to start having a social media detox every night. When you are up on social media and your smart phone or tablet all night, reading and commenting, it can keep you alert and wired. If you are finding it hard to fall asleep, then try to create a digital detox routine to help.

It's also best to start dimming lights, turning off the TV, and creating a calm space. You want to start unwinding before you have to go to bed, so do calming, relaxing things like a warm shower or bath and gentle, nurturing, self-love activities.

Create your bedroom to have soft colours, and take any TVs out. Declutter it and turn it into a calming, peaceful sanctuary. I don't have a TV in my room, and I don't even like to sleep with my smart phone next to my bed. All of these things keep you magnetically connected. I went to one of Australia's leading wellness retreats, and when you stay there, they don't have TVs in the rooms. I do think this makes a huge difference. Along with the energy of your room, if your room is soft, calm, and peaceful, it will help prepare you for a good night's sleep.

Also, because sleep is the most important thing when it comes to our health and well-being, it's good to check in with how your bed is making you feel. Is it comfortable and letting you have a good night's sleep, or is it too old and so uncomfortable that you are tossing and turning? So many things come into play when it comes to getting a good night's sleep, but preparation and having a set routine so that your body naturally gets used to your bedtime routine is key.

Drink Lots of Water

I always carry water with me everywhere I go.

Experts recommend drinking around eight glasses (or two litres) per day, however this is only a guide and can be different for everyone. I find when I am drinking enough water, I feel a lot better and less lethargic. I have more energy, and it also prevents me from overeating. I found sometimes when I wasn't drinking enough water, I would think I was hungry, but I was thirsty instead.

When you are at home, drink out of a cup to help prevent those bottle upper lip wrinkles and lines. Also, drinking out of a cup helps reduce any chemicals or toxins that come from drinking out of a plastic bottle.

I recommend that wherever you go, carry a BPA bottle of water with you; filtered water is best if you can. BPA water bottles reduce the chemicals you are exposed to when drinking water.

Wherever I go, I always carry a bottle of water with me. Drinking water will make you feel hydrated and healthy, and it also will do wonders for your skin.

Be Kind

Today I woke up and decided to be kind to everyone else, including myself.

Smile and do little random acts of kindness. I created my very first online blog as a random act of kindness, so I could share the things I loved with the hope it would make others feel good.

I truly believed if I gave more than I got, the universe would have my back and amazing things would happen. I never wanted my blog to be all about the money. I chose to start my blog so it could help others. I didn't make it for money and greed. These are the same spiritual principles I have to this very day.

Throughout my day-to-day life, I love doing little random acts of kindness. It might be something as simple as asking someone if she also wants a coffee, knowing that I am going to be going across the road to get one. Or it could be seeing someone struggling with carrying a couple of boxes and then asking her if I can help. I may see an old lady unsure about how to use a certain machine, and I stop to ask if she needs any help. Whenever I see someone who might need a hand, I feel a calling to help and serve others.

When you become present and spirituality connected, you will start to notice opportunities and moments when you can do little random acts of kindness. Before you know it, you will also be a light worker on Mother Earth.

Being kind is one of the best ways to feel present and spiritually connected. Doing something nice for someone else is the greatest gift you could ever give. When someone is going through a hard time, it's always nice to be able to offer any help. I know personally that people who have always reached out to offer help to me during difficult times have made the biggest difference, and even if I didn't need their help, it was simply them expressing their love, light, and kindness, which made all the difference.

As a light worker on Mother Earth, I truly believe life is all about being kind to yourself and others well. Doing random acts of kindness will make you feel good. and helping others feels good too. I truly believe it's great for your health, happiness, and wellness.

Being kind makes an everlasting connection. I remember everyone who has ever been kind to me—that's how powerful being kind is. You can't change the other people choose to live their lives but you can change the way you choose to live your life, so be kind.

When you make a shift to being kind, you start to radiate positive energy full of love and light. What you give out is what you get back, so being kind every day will make all the difference to what you bring to yourself and the world.

Of course, there will be times when no matter how hard you try, someone will still choose to be unkind. When this happens, do your best to always be kind and live your own life with kindness.

Be Grateful

I am grateful every single waking day. I choose to be grateful in every possible way.

Be grateful every single day. You can practice gratitude each day by writing down three things for which you are grateful. Throughout the day, become fully present and notice things that you are grateful for; you can express this out loud to someone else or do it within.

When you become grateful, you realise how amazing your life truly is. Being grateful is a beautiful, gentle reminder of what you already have, and it will start to teach you are enough and have enough. A grateful heart and soul will change the way you feel and see everything whilst on Mother Earth.

Self-care with Skincare

Love yourself through self-care.

I believe skincare starts from within. That's why when people ask me what my skincare routine is, I always say I eat lots of fresh, natural, unprocessed foods. I truly believe that helps with radiant, glowing, healthy, natural skin.

I love to eat fresh raspberries, and also I eat healthy fats like avocado. Since introducing even two healthy foods, I have seen a massive difference in my skin.

I drink lots of water and also credit practicing yoga, exercising, meditating, smiling, self-love, being kind to others, and visiting day spas for facials as part of my self-care skincare routine.

A lot of people ask me what my skincare tips are, so here they are.

Wake up each day and wash your face using chemical-free, natural skincare products. Cleanse, exfoliate, tone, and moisturize your face with face cream. Dab under the eyes with a suitable eye cream.

Make the time when you brush your teeth to clean your skin, or do your daily morning routine in the bath to save time.

Make sure you remove all your make-up with a suitable make-up cleaner or natural cloth. Never go to bed with your make-up on.

Do your bedtime skincare routine again: cleanse, exfoliate, tone, moisturize. To save time, keep your cleanser and exfoliator in the shower so that when you have a shower, you can wash your face, and it's done.

Make cleaning your skin a daily thing and use natural skincare products that are vegan-friendly, plant-based, and organic if possible—and Australian made, of course.

If you want to look after your whole skin, go for it and try a body scrub to exfoliate your skin twice a week. When you get out of the shower, take the time to lather your skin with a beautiful body cream or oil.

Connect to yourself through this beautiful self-care practice. Love your body and skin the way it is.

Create a self-care skincare routine that suits you. Use products that don't have any chemicals in them.

Eat lots of fresh, healthy fruits, vegetables, as well as plant-based and natural unprocessed foods. This will help nourish your skin from within. Drink loads of water and get your beauty sleep. Take a vitamin C tablet to help boost your skin.

Make time when you can to have a facial from a day spa to give your skin a really deep cleanse, and to work specifically on your own skin needs.

I turn forty this year, and I have never had any Botox or cosmetic surgery I have also loved being a natural, down-to-earth Aussie beauty.

I've never been one to wear a lot of make-up, and I now love empowering other girls and women to love being comfortable in their own skin. Yes, that even means leaving the house make-up free!

Love Yourself No Matter What

All the love you need comes from within. Love yourself unconditionally.

The most important relationship is the one you have with yourself. We can spend so much time looking for love outside of us that we can disconnect from our truth, which is love.

I grew up reading fairy tales as a kid. From them I learnt that when you meet someone else and they decide they love you, then you will be in love and feel love.

If I could rewrite the fairy tale as my older, wiser self, it would be this: All the love you need comes from within, and princes will come and go. Don't get hung up thinking that love comes only from someone else, because love has to come from yourself.

Loving yourself first else may not come easily if you have been brought up to love everyone else before yourself. However, loving yourself first before anyone else is key.

Love Yourself from Within

Do you stand in front of the mirror and love what you see and who you are? Or do you look in the mirror and start picking body image to pieces?

I have personally had my own struggles when it has come to loving myself unconditionally.

I use to love reading the dolly magazine, and at the time when I used to look at the cover, I would see this happy, pretty Aussie girl living the dream.

I saw that I could enter a competition to become the face of the magazine, and all I had to do was send in a picture of myself (a portrait and full body). The winner could earn amazing prizes and even a modelling contract, as well as be on the cover of the magazine. I was so excited.

I was a teenager living in a small country town, with three pubs, one post office, and no street lights. I honestly would have done anything to travel the world. When I found out anyone could enter and didn't have to be with a modelling agency, I got even more excited.

I sent off my entry and waited with anticipation to later buy the magazine in order to discover what girls had been short-listed.

The first thing I noticed wasn't what they looked like, but what dress size they were and how they were all skinnier than me by a dress size or more. Of course, I automatically thought that the reason I didn't get picked was that I was too big in size. As a kid, I couldn't process why, because when I looked at the girls' faces, they all looked the same, happy and smiling, but smaller and skinnier in size. That's what I then started to see that when looking at magazines or TV, only girls who were skinny got the opportunity to be on them. It didn't matter where I looked; when it came to the media, I couldn't find anyone who looked like me and had my body shape or was a size ten. I grew up in the days when skinny was really in.

Even though I didn't win the competition, I wasn't a sore loser. I thought those who did win had that skinny, lanky fashion model look with no hips look. Let's face it: the likes of Miranda Kerr got discovered in the CoverGirl competition, and she was from an Aussie farm, so they definitely were looking for supermodel contenders. But as a young Aussie teenager, I couldn't process this at the time.

Even after not becoming a CoverGirl, I still was fascinated with modelling. I think it was mainly because I loved having my photo taken, and the idea of travel and the opportunities that came with it. To me, it sounded great. I went on to do more casting calls, only to walk away with direct, face-to-face feedback that I really needed to lose weight, a whole dress size. Then when I was a size eight, I should come back and try out again. Another time it was because I had too big a chest, and they only wanted flat-chested girls. But prior to the casting calls, I didn't know any of this, and I grew up in the era when nothing was PC.

As a natural size ten and natural size 10DD. I started to learn I didn't fit into what people were looking for. When I received the feedback about my body weight, shape, and size, I would take a big gulp, put on a heartbroken smile, and say thanks. I would walk out feeling like crap, and I must admit over time it had a negative impact on me.

On a positive note, during that time I was told by top professional modelling agencies that I was perfect for photographic work and TV commercial work. With Instagram being so big now, I get to do photo shoots as a healthy, curvy size ten. No one seems to mind in this day and age what size I am. I do think Instagram is great for any girl of any shape or size to express herself. I should point out all of those giving me negative body image feedback were not the best modelling agencies at the time. There were so many out there always doing casting calls.

Getting knocked back personally affected me because I was a lot younger and was easily influenced by others. I thought that I did have to lose weight like they had suggested. I went through a stage where I trained my butt off and ate a really strict diet. I dropped down to a size nine and then a size eight, but all that happened was I got run down and sick, and I became unhealthy from within.

I decided to give up the idea of being part of the modelling and fashion industry. I would find a new industry where I could be myself. That was when I thought about what I truly loved. Exercise made me good, and it didn't matter what shape or size I was; all I had to do was take a class, motivate and inspire others to exercise, have fun, and feel good whilst listening to music. I got paid to exercise and even had free gym membership, so I was excited. I started teaching aerobics when cassettes were in, and I had to write my own classes. I loved doing grapevines, and I still love doing them today.

I found every time I taught a class, I should be really pumped and full of energy. I loved seeing everyone else having fun too, so for me it helped with developing a positive body image. I learnt that all I had to do to feel good was exercise, eat a balanced diet, and have fun. I was fine just the way I was. No one ever once said I didn't fit in. When it comes to the fitness industry, if anything I was run off my feet, teaching back-to-back classes or six classes a week whilst still holding down a full-time job. To this day I am grateful that I chose to be part of the fitness industry instead of trying to maintain an unhealthy weight just to fit into the modelling and fashion industry.

I started practicing yoga, and I do believe this helped me make peace within when it came to my own body image. I found a way to love myself unconditionally, and I learnt to respect my body for how it was and for what it could do for me. I learn to self-accept and self-love my body. I learnt that I was fine just the way I was, and there was nothing wrong with my body shape or size. I think that as girls, we are under constant body image pressure. We allow ourselves to be. I work in social media and have been online for ten years now. When I first started out blogging, no one even knew what I looked like for years, or even my name; it was all about storytelling and connecting to the reader through words. If anything, the photos were of the spa resort and not myself. Fast forward to now, and everything in the online world is about photos, photography, and looks. Bloggers are seen as models, models are seen as bloggers, and it's all a bit messy as to who writes for a regular blog and who just posts modelling photos.

Nevertheless, I have learnt it's best not to compare yourself with anyone other than yourself, especially because when I was growing up as a kid, we only had a certain amount of magazines. Now, Instagram alone has five hundred million users signed up, so if you start comparing yourself with other girls or people online, and then you start comparing the amount of your followers or likes to someone else's, you compare your own body shape and size and make comparisons. It can become an unhealthy thing, and before you know it, you might start to question your weight, body shape, and size. Then you might start to look at yourself in an unkind, unloving way.

What you can do if you love being online and looking at photos as much as me is to always appreciate every girl for who she is. Stop comparing your own body shape or size with anyone else's. Appreciate that every girl, woman, and person is beautiful just like you. Appreciate a person in a photo for who she is, don't cast any judgement, and appreciate the creative work and personality that has gone into it. Look at photos now like you would at an art gallery, where you stand back and admire it. Sometimes you might not be able to make sense of it, but that's okay; it's a work of art, so you embrace it and admire it for what it is.

I have found that through my own yoga practice I was able to connect to my true inner self. That helped me let go of negative body-image influences from the past, and it helped me heal from within. Every time I looked in the mirror and a negative thought came up about my body shape or size, I was able to become the observer of my own thoughts. Instead of identifying with it, I would let it rise and fall. When I created space within I was then able to choose my own identity and what I wanted to identify with. I learnt through my own spiritual practice that only loving thoughts are my truth; any self-hate and negative thoughts no longer served me, and I chose to stop identifying with them.

When I looked in the mirror in the morning, I started to take on my negative thoughts. I wouldn't identify with them, and I would then send myself a loving thought. I continued the process over and over until one day when I looked in the mirror, I no longer picked my own body self or image to pieces. It was the most liberating feeling, and I felt that I had finally conquered my body image struggle.

I became my own best friend and surrendered to what no longer served my highest good. The struggle that I had going on inside for all those years was finally over. It felt so good, and I felt the love within. It freed up so much good energy and took away so much negative energy that I couldn't believe it. From then on, I wanted to help other girls love themselves unconditionally, accepting who they were and how they were even whilst they were trying to achieve their weight-loss goals, which can be one of the hardest things to do when you are trying to lose weight, looking at yourself in the mirror, and hating what you see. However, the more you can love what you see, the better you will feel.

I am not going to pretend that making peace within is easy. Even when you make peace within, you are only human and are still going to have negative thoughts pop up. However, when you start to create space within and connect to your true inner spirit, you know that negative thoughts about you aren't your truth. By knowing that, you can then send yourself kind, loving, positive thoughts every time a negative thought show up. This will allow you to love yourself instead of buying into a negative thought that is not your truth.

When you start to actively practice self-care and self-love, you still start to feel better. In time when you look at yourself in the mirror, it won't be an inner struggle or self-hate; it will be simply you looking at yourself in the mirror. Continue waking up and getting ready to brush your teeth. Head off to meditate and then set your intentions. Go exercise and then live your authentic passions and dreams. Nourish yourself, practice yoga, smile, and be kind. In this way, instead of feeling like crap from beating yourself up from within, you are starting your day in a positive, loving way.

I think that each and every girl is unique. We are authentic, and there is only one spirit that lives within us. That is what makes up more than our body shape or size.

I also think that in a world that is always online, it's important to make sure those you follow or have in your immediate life make you feel good. It's important to understand what someone brings to the world, and to not follow someone just for her body image, shape, size, or looks. We are so much more than our physical selves, and our spiritual selves are more powerful than the body and mind. Always look well beyond someone's body shape and size.

Be kind and compassionate towards yourself, and be accepting of who you are and how you are. Be kind and compassionate to other people too. When you learn to love yourself from within, it makes you feel happy, healthy, confident, kind, loving, and caring.

Roll out your yoga mat, because when you practice yoga, you connect with your higher self. It helps you overcome any obstacles and body image issues.

Other ways to work on self-love are by writing beautiful things about yourself, journaling, counselling, writing your own positive self-love mantras, giving yourself a big hug when you need it, going easy on yourself when you need it, and always practicing self-care and self-love. Do little self-love things like taking a long bath, spending time in Mother Nature, having a massage, and loving yourself unconditionally. Doing anything that nurtures your body, mind, and soul. will help you connect with your loving self and the spirit within. All the love you need comes from within when you take the time to love and care for yourself.

When you love yourself, your whole world changes. You discover that you are beautiful along with every other girl around the world, and that there is no need for comparison or competition over body image.

If you want to become your healthiest and happiest self, making peace within and loving yourself unconditionally is key. When you look in a mirror, don't buy into any unkind, negative thoughts that come up. Simply take deep breaths and let them rise and fall. Take your negative self-talk or self-hate thoughts head-on. Look at yourself in the mirror and send yourself kind, loving thoughts, which only come from a place of love because that is your truth.

Remember that you are fine the way you are this is your truth, so live it. There is nothing wrong with your body image, shape, size, or looks. Change your story within and love yourself unconditionally. I know you can do it.

Your truth is that you are beautiful just the way you are. Even when people tell you otherwise, your truth is always that you are beautiful. You simply didn't know then what you know now.

Become the Observer

Not every thought you have about yourself is true. Only choose to listen and accept loving thoughts, because that is your truth.

We all have negative and positive thoughts that happen within. Only we can hear our own thoughts—unless you write them down or say them out loud.

As girls, we hate when other people do or say nasty things about us. Being nasty to ourselves or others doesn't serve our highest good.

When it comes to our own internal thoughts, we might have our own inner bitch thoughts about ourselves. Then identify with negative thoughts from within. When we start latching on to every thought that is happening inside us, it becomes the way we feel, see, and become. We then start to disconnect from our true inner spirit.

We can sometimes think that every thought that is coming from within is actually coming from our own inner spirit because it's coming up as a thought. But when you connect to your own inner spirit within, and it speaks, and you make the time to listen, it will only come from a place of true love and light. Your own kind, loving inner spirit never wants to hate you, harm you, or make you sick. It only wants to love you, help you, guide you, and make you feel happy, abundant, healthy. It will give you all the love, light, and support you need.

When you practice meditation, you will learn to focus your attention inwards onto your breath, and you will learn to become the observer. You will learn to let your own internal thoughts rise and fall, and you will not determine whether it's a good thought or a bad thought. You will simply acknowledge that it's no more than a thought, and you will learn to let it rise and fall.

Practicing meditation will help by creating space within. You will become the observer and will be able to understand that not every thought is real or going to happen. Not every thought serves your highest good, and you not everything you think is true. You are more than your thoughts.

When thoughts, feelings, and emotions come from a place of love, light, and kindness, you know you are connected with your inner spirit. When they don't serve your highest good, you know it's in your best interest to become the observer and let your thoughts rise and fall.

You do have the power within to change the way you feel. By becoming an observer, you can connect with your true inner self and always choose love over hate.

Self-love Sunday

Love yourself unconditionally.

I learnt about self-love Sunday thanks to my beautiful mum. When I was a kid, she would make Sunday a day of self-care and self-love.

She used to sit on the front patio's top stair and paint her toenails. She'd practice self-love by reading a book and doing easy, gentle things to take care of herself. She didn't do this as a one-off here and there—she did self-care and self-love every single Sunday. Naturally, I followed in her footsteps. Now, through my Spa It Girl blog (www.spaitgirl.com), we celebrate Spa It Girl Self-love Sunday every week. It's such a beautiful way to focus on your own self, give yourself self-love and self-care, and accept that it's okay if you want to lie on the couch and do nothing. You can do so because Sunday is also a day of rest.

Letting going of having to be a human doing and becoming a human being allows you to focus on letting go of your to-do list and all expectations. Sometimes all we need is to simply be and to relax.

I love how practicing self-love Sunday doesn't have to cost the earth. You can do simple little things. Sit in a beautiful chair and drink a nice cup of tea. Read a feel-good book. Watch a chick flick that that makes you laugh. Have a nice, long shower or a relaxing bath. Go to the day spa. Get a relaxing massage. Paint your own toenails. Buy yourself a bunch of fresh flowers.

Lie by the pool and go for a swim. Take a beautiful walk in the outdoors to appreciate Mother Nature. Watch the sunrise or sunset.

Practice an easy, gentle yoga flow. Meditate. Pop on a facemask. Listen to some beautiful music to soothe your soul. Lie on the couch, relax, and do nothing.

Sit on the beach and listen to the waves of the ocean. Feel the sun on your skin.

Let go of your mobile phone and disconnect from the world. Spend time alone or with those you love. Forget about social media and news feeds. Start focusing on loving yourself unconditionally and from within.

Spa It Girl's self-love Sundays will always make you feel well. I invite you to join me in this beautiful self-love practice every Sunday, along with every other Spa It Girl from around the world.

Choose Your Energy

Surround yourself with those who love you and support you.

Everything is energy, and people and things can give off either positive energy or negative energy. It's important to tune in to how every person and thing makes you feel within.

When you become aware and spiritually present, you will be able to pick up if someone in your life brings you positive energy that lifts you and makes you feel safe, supported, and loved, or if someone brings you negative energy, brings you down, and makes you feel sick and unsettled.

Life is precious, and you need to do what is best for you. If you know within that someone doesn't make you feel good, or you feel that you don't energetically connect, it's okay to cut your ties and get rid of toxic people within your life. That way you can become your happiest and healthiest spiritual self.

I don't just choose my energy when it comes to people. I choose to surround myself with positive energy in just about anything and everything I do. The more spiritual awakened I become, the more I can tune into energy and what it brings to not only this world but my own internal world.

In my home, I choose to surround myself with beautiful colours like turquoise, green, and pretty pink. I choose feel-good signs like "Love" and "Believe." I have beautiful yoga mats, a cushion that says "Good Vibes," my beautiful Spa It Girl logo postcards (because the Spa it Girl brand logo is just so feel good and pretty), self-help books, my yellow Buddha bookends, candles, my gold Buddha that I personally painted, happy photos of my family and friends, beautiful tea cups—you name it. I have selected everything for my own home because it makes me feel good, and it brings positive energy with it.

I pick everything and truly believe items have been guided to me through my own intuition. Through my higher self, I know that no matter what, I have done my best to create the most positive energy and space. Then I do my best to make sure I only invite the same kind of energy into my private space.

I do believe practicing yoga or meditating helps with becoming spiritually aware and being able to pick up on energy a lot easier. When you are with someone who radiates negative energy, she will instantly make you feel bad and bring down your energy levels. Something won't sit right in your stomach, and well after she has gone, the negative energy can make you sick. Her negative energy then becomes part of your own energy field.

Negative energy can linger, and that's when you have to clear and remove the negative energy from your own field by doing simple, effective energy-clearing techniques. They can come from mediations for clearing negative energy, tapping techniques, or listening to music. There are just so many options.

Energy comes from everything, from the TV you watch to movies, music, and what you read. Everything is an energy, so if it's a feel-good energy, that's what you are going to feel and experience. If it's a negative, horrible, fearful, nasty energy, then that is what you are going to feel.

My best advice is to become in tune with how things make you truly feel. If something doesn't feel quite right, there is a reason for that. Even if you bought a movie that you thought was going to be okay, and you find out fifteen minutes into it that it's horrible and making you feel bad, my advice is to forget about how much money it cost. Simply eject it because you don't need to take on that type of negative energy.

Choose to experience and attract energy that makes you feel good. Tune into the energy you want to feel and receive. You can attract anything you put your mind to, so be mindful to always choose things that are going to make you feel good, loved, happy, safe, comfortable, and at peace.

The energy you choose to connect to is really important if you want to feel good within. Positive energy will lift you up, and negative energy will bring you down. You may discover there is someone in your life who isn't like-minded, and she brings you down with her negative energy. Once you start tuning in to energy fields and how other people or things affect your own energy field, you will discover a lot more about a person—well beyond her overall looks, status, or job title. The energy a person carries speaks louder than words.

Think of it like this: You are walking down a road, and you have a choice. You can have your earphones in to listen to beautiful, feel-good, happy music that will lift you up and inspire you to do your best, be your best, and be proud of who you are and how you are. The energy energises you and makes you feel that everything is great; you feel safe.

The other choice is that you can put in your earphones and listen to horrible, negative music full of doom and gloom that brings your energy level down, makes you feel unsettled and unsafe, and makes you feel sick within.

Choosing your energy is important, and that's why I invite you to tune in and start working out what makes you feel good and what makes you feel like crap. It's as simple as that.

You will know off the top of your head those people in your life who make you feel good and those people who don't. That gives you an indication of who radiates positive energy or negative energy in your own energy field.

I don't tend to watch TV because I don't want to get caught up in all of the drama it has to offer. I find it so peaceful to have it off. If you ever came to my place, you would instead find soothing, relaxing, day spa music playing, or some kind of feel-good music. I love how music can inspire and bring an abundance of positive energy.

Do your best to connect to as much positive energy that the universe and world has to bring. You have the power to choose the right energy for you and your own health and wellness.

Choose those people who bring positive energy into your life and who want to be your friend because they truly love you, support you, and want to see the best for you. Cut ties with those who don't make you feel good, who bring your own energy levels down, and who don't serve your highest good.

Be a Spa It Girl

I love visiting spas and having spa treatments. They make me feel so good. I think making time for yourself to care for yourself is an absolute must if you want to feel happy and healthy within.

Life can be so busy, and we can find ourselves always being on the go. Sometimes we need to stop and take time out for ourselves. That way we can relax, let go of every single thing, and simply be.

I chose to follow my own authentic passion and dreams for visiting and reviewing luxury day spas, regardless of what anyone else thought. I am now one of the world's most well-known luxury spa travel reviewers and bloggers. I'm the founder of Spa It Girl, an online spa and wellness site and global community (www.spaitgirl.com). I'm the it girl of the spa industry, and I absolutely love it.

I love visiting spas so much that becoming one of the world's leading spa bloggers is a dream come true. I never gave up on my dream despite others saying no to my ideas, my vision, and what I wanted to become.

I first started visiting day spas when I was working in the corporate world. I worked as a personal assistant for one of

Australia's leading CEOs, whom I loved to bits and who inspired me in every possible way. I learnt so much from her. She was the ultimate girl boss, that's for sure: strong, clever, an inspirational leader, a motivator, and a go-getter who never stopped. She worked her butt off, and so did I.

I was working and living in the city, and at the time I felt like I needed to get away to unwind, destress, relax, and have a break. I couldn't get away to go on a holiday because work was just so busy. I decided to book myself into a luxury day spa that I had recently learnt about because the brochure had been sent to my CEO. At the time, I had to open and read all of her mail. After reading about the spa and what it had to offer, I booked myself to have a spa treatment on Saturday afternoon. From the moment I walked through the luxury spa door, I instantly switched off and felt relaxed. It was like I'd left all my cares, worries, and to-do list at the door. It was a complete shift in energy and focus instantly.

I then went through the whole luxury day spa experience, from putting on my fluffy spa bath robe to sipping on a nice cup of relaxation tea, to using all of the spa's facilities. I loved using their spa bath and feeling all the jets on my back and upper shoulders.

I had a relaxation massage, and I loved how I was able to fully surrender, letting down all my guards to relax, unwind, and restore my body, mind, and spirit. At the end, I felt whole again. I was well rested, not stressed, and relaxed and happy. I knew I had found something special, an ancient ritual of spa therapy that would see me through these crazy, busy, modern times.

Visiting a day spa made me feel so good within that when I left, I felt like a totally new person. It was so transformational that from that moment onwards, I knew that was all I wanted to do: visit luxury day spas, receive spa therapy, and then write about it to share my personal experiences. I hoped that if it made me feel good, it would help others feel good. I felt so passion and driven, and I wanted to get other people to experience the health and wellness benefits that visiting a day spa could bring. It was like I had discovered the greatest form of therapy on earth, spa therapy. To this day, I am just as passionate, if not more so, about visiting spas, having spa treatments, getting spa therapy, and sharing my experiences to inspire others to try being a Spa It Girl.

Being a Spa It Girl is all about feeling good, visiting day spas, and taking time out for you so that you can nurture yourself from within and restore your own health and wellness through spa therapy. I love how I can walk in off a busy city street with the biggest to-do list, but as soon as I open the day spa door, everything changes for me. I go from doing to simply being.

Visiting a luxury day spa is one of the most peaceful, tranquil places on earth, besides Mother Nature.

It truly is a place of serenity. I love all of the beautiful spa wellness rituals and how every single day spa I have ever visited is authentic and unique. They all have their own passions, beliefs, and practices. That's another reason why I love visiting spas and being the founder of Spa It Girl: each day is never the same, and I'm always trying and learning new spa, wellness, and spiritual healing techniques, along with always meeting amazing managers, therapists and those within the industry. I also have my own loyal Spa It Girl readers who brighten every single day. My Spa It Girl blog readers and followers have my back, and they love and support my work. I am so grateful because they make me love Spa It Girl every single day.

I love drinking the day spa's relaxing tea of the day; it's one of my Spa It Girl must-dos. I also love going in early before my spa treatment and using the spa facilities. I love having a spa bath because it is so relaxing, soothes my soul, and helps release any built-up tension. It gets me relaxed and ready for my spa treatment. I like to spend a little bit of time relaxing in the relaxation lounges and chairs before and after my spa treatments.

When I am being a Spa It Girl, I am totally present. I have found that visiting a luxury day spa is one place where I totally surrender.

I love how being a Spa It Girl has nothing to do with the way you look. It's not about your dress size or body shape. It doesn't matter if have on make-up or fancy clothes. You simply need to be yourself, let go, put on a comfy bathrobe, and disconnect with everything in your world in order to reconnect with your true inner self. Being a Spa It Girl is all about self-love and self-care. It's about taking time out for your own body, mind, and soul and giving yourself a much-needed break. It's about letting go to things that no longer serve your highest good.

Being a Spa It Girl is all about allowing and making the time to heal. When you receive spa therapy, it helps you emotionally, physically, mentally, and spiritually.

I love having a massage. It makes me feel so good inside and out, and it always helps with working out my tight spots and knots. It's so great for stress and helps you to relax. I think having a massage is a must for everyone. A lot of people in Australia are heading over to Bali so they can receive spa treatments every day whilst on their holidays. If that is not possible for you, then I encourage you to try your local day spa. Depending on your budget, find a spa therapy beauty school and take part in their free or discounted spa therapist student practical days. It's a great way to receive spa therapy from those who are passionate about the spa industry.

I am a big fan of having facials. Having a facial is part of my Spa It Girl way of life. I find it does wonders for my skin. I tend to go for the deep-cleansing facial because when you visit a day spa, they do such a good job. Now that I am turning forty this year, I have more recently been having anti-ageing facials. I have never had Botox or any cosmetic surgery, and I have always believed in being my natural self. I credit being a Spa It Girl, visiting day spas, and having facials when it comes to maintaining my healthy, glowing skin. A lot of people think I am in my early thirties, and when I tell them I going to be turning forty, they can't believe it.

What I love about having a facial is not only is it a great way to get rid of built-up dead skin, but it helps with blocked and clogged pores. It's so relaxing, and I love that therapeutic side of things.

If you want to improve your own skin and work on your skin needs, then having a facial by a trained spa therapist is great because she can tailor the facial to suit what your skin needs. I am always amazed at how much I learn about my own skin and skincare after I have a facial with a trained spa therapist.

It doesn't really matter what you choose to have from a spa menu. The chances are any spa treatment you have is going to make you feel good. Spa therapy is so therapeutic and healing, and it's great for your overall health and well-being. I always knew it was more than a beauty treatment, and that is why ever since I started writing about day spas, it was all about the how it made me feel and how it great it is for my health, wellness, body, mind, and soul.

If you want to change the way you feel, then I invite you to be a Spa It Girl and book in for a beautiful spa treatment.

Before you go to your spa treatment, make a note of how you feel. Then make a note of how you feel when you come out. compare the two; you should notice a big different.

I believe everyone deserves to feel good from within, and receiving spa therapy and being a Spa It Girl is key.

I created my blog Spa It Girl because I love visiting spas and the way they make me feel. Because visiting a spa made me feel so good, I wanted to share this with others so they could feel good too.

I also created the mantra of, "You are the it girl at the spa, and all you need to do to feel good is spa it, girl." In other words, go to the spa!

Throughout my travels, I have met so many amazing spa therapists, and I believe that they are healers and the world needs them. I am always grateful and respect the amazing work they do.

Once you start visiting day spas and having spa treatments, you will discover just how good it feels. Being a Spa It Girl and visiting a day spa is the greatest self-care and self-love thing you could ever do. It makes you feel so well in body, mind, and spirit. After you have visited a spa and received a spa treatment once, you will want to experience more. I love spas so much, and I hope you love receiving spa therapy as much as I do. I believe spa therapy is a form of healing. If you want to make peace within, love yourself, and practice self-love and self-care, then visiting a day spa and having a treatment is a must.

When I go on holidays, or even for mini weekend breaks, I only ever stay at places that offer spa therapy. If you want to get some ideas of spas to visit, then go to <u>www.spaitgirl.com</u>. I personally pick and review some of the world's best spas and spa destinations, and I love sharing how it truly is and how it makes me feel.

I also love that through our Spa It Girl global community, any Spa It Girl can share her own inspirations. We also have Spa It Girl contributors, with experiences being shared. Spa It Girl has grown so much beyond my wildest dreams, but I love how Spa It Girl is not just about me. I truly love sharing other Spa It Girls' inspirations, as well as unearthing other spas and helping those who love spas and wellness as much as I do. In this way, they can have their own thoughts and feelings be heard.

Being a Spa It Girl means so much to me, so I wanted to personally want to thank each and every one of our Spa It Girls. If you are brand-new to my Spa It Girl global feel-good movement, I want to welcome you.

On that note, make time to visit a day spa when you can, and enjoy being your own Spa It Girl. I can't wait to see you rocking it in your spa robe and feeling so happy, healthy, relaxed, and spiritually connected within.

If you are on Instagram, be sure to share your Spa It Girl moment by taking a photo at the beautiful day spa. Use #iamaspaitgirl and tag @Spaitgirl. I can't wait to see your happy, glowing #iamaspaitgirl smile.

Being a Spa It Girl is all about self-love and self-care. I invite you to give being a Spa It Girl a go it a go; it will help you become your happiest and healthiest self.

Self-belief

Everything starts from within and through self-belief. When you believe in yourself, anything and everything is possible. Every time your fear or doubt kicks in, let the thought and feeling rise and fall, and always believe in yourself.

I wouldn't be living my dreams and writing this book if I didn't believe in myself and have self-belief. Throughout my whole life, I have always had setbacks, knockbacks, and more nos then yeses. I've had plenty of things that have gone pear-shaped and situations that have not been ideal. But with every setback, my one constant remained: self-belief.

When I wanted to become a luxury spa travel reviewer, so many people said no to my passions, dreams, and ideas. There wasn't even a job to apply for, so I created my own blog. That way I could follow my own passion, love, and dream. I started writing, reviewing and blogging about luxury day spas. If I waited for someone else to create the job I wanted to do, or to give me the actual opportunity, I might very well still be waiting! I wouldn't be living my true, authentic self, with my passions and dreams. I am now the founder of Spa It Girl, an online spa and wellness blog and global community.

To this day, I do luxury spa travel review for the love of it. I still write, review, and blog for the love of it, even though blogging has headed towards the modelling side of things with endorsing products. I still love connecting with my Spa It Girl blog followers, meeting and connecting with like-minded people, and sharing my love and the things that make me feel good, in the hope that it will make others feel good.

I wouldn't still be online had I not believed in myself and been my true, authentic self.

When you are a creative soul and a spiritual being, everything you do comes from within. You learn to trade love, light, and kindness. Miracles do happen thanks to the universe.

Had I not had self-belief, I wouldn't be living my dreams today. I had a mantra: "No one knows me as well as I know myself. I know I can do this, and I am going to do it." Even if someone who had the power to make my dream happen said no, I would remind myself that was okay; it was not meant to be, and the person couldn't see or feel what I felt. I kept pursuing my dreams because it made me feel good, and I knew it would make others feel good. Why would I ever let anyone else's no stop me?

Self-belief is a powerful energy, and once you have mastered it and truly believe in yourself, you can do or be anything.

You can live your dreams. Things you have always dreamed of but thought you could never do start happening naturally, when the timing is right and you are ready.

You do have to have a lot of self-belief when you are starting something from nothing, from your heart and soul. I personally didn't have any media contacts, I wasn't a professional model, I didn't have a university degree, and I didn't live in Sydney (which was seen as the coolest place to live in Australia). I had no money, no financial backing, and not even someone in either media or business to guide me. I had no man or partner to financially back me up. It was just me and one very big Spa It Girl dream.

I could go on and on about all the things I didn't have, but the most important thing I *did* have was self-belief. With self-belief, you can do anything and everything.

I am now recognised in the spa industry as the it girl. The fashion industry always had it girls, so I decided the spa industry deserved to have one too. That is what I created and became. I also wanted to create an online spa wellness and lifestyle blog, and I am the founder of Spa It Girl (www. spaitgirl.com), which is read all around the world. This year I just got named as one of Australia's Top Fifty Influencers. Having my love and passion for spas and my Spa It Girl way of life out there is really exciting.

I wanted to create an online community for all girls around the world to connect as Spa It Girls, we so we could share our love for visiting day spas and living healthy, happy, spiritual lives. I wanted to create an online global Spa It Girl community so that we could all love, support, and empower one another.

All of this didn't happen overnight. It took a lot of self-belief and a lot of hours working for free. That didn't bother me one little bit because I started my blog for the love of it, not for the money.

I've been online for about ten years now, writing, reviewing, blogging, and creating my own authentic, creative content. I have seen people come and go, and quite often the ones who start something to make money come and go. It's always the passionate ones who stay.

I am only human, and of course I have made plenty of mistakes. However, I don't see this as a failure. I see this as learning, development, and growth. I allow the universe to guide me in so many ways, and my self-belief has been my one constant; it has got me through some of the really tough times.

I believe you have to have your own back in everything you do. If you don't have your own back, then who will? Just like self-love, self-belief has to come from within. When you have your own back, the universe has your back. When you co-create with the universe, that's when the real magic happens.

When you come from a place of love and light, and you want to show up each day and serve others, then the universe will guide you and help make things happen.

Never give up on your own personal dreams and the person you want to become. Never give up on how you want to feel and what you want to overcome.

Have faith in your own ability, be patient, and work towards your own personal goals and dreams. I know with self-belief, you can achieve anything. When you back yourself, the universe has your back. When you stay focused, even if others doubt your own abilities, remember that only you know how you truly feel inside. If you are truly passionate about something, or something means so much to you, then never give up on how it makes you feel. If I'd listened to what others people had to say about my idea to become a luxury spa travel reviewer, I wouldn't be living my dreams and Spa It Girl wouldn't exist. Remember that if you want to make something happen, you can as long as you have self-belief and believe in yourself, regardless of what anyone else thinks.

When what you want to achieve comes from within and is your true passion and dream, it comes from your own heart and soul. You can make anything happen with self-belief.

It's only when you are trying to live someone else's passion and calling it your own that you come unstuck. Stay true to your own authentic self and always believe in yourself.

Do Things That Make You Feel Good

Choose to do things that make you feel good.

This is my go-to mantra, and it's how I live my life. Each day when I wake up, I choose to do things that make me feel good. It's now my life purpose to feel good and to make others feel good.

I struggled in my early twenties to make sense of what my life's purpose was. I felt so confused that I didn't know what to do. I wasn't working in my dream job. I had an administration job that wasn't my true, authentic passion; it was simply something I fell into because it was seen as being a good corporate job. Even though I was working a part-time job as an aerobics instructor and working in the fitness industry, I still felt confused as to what I truly wanted to do. I often thought about studying at university like everyone else, but it didn't call for me. It didn't get me excited from within.

It wasn't until I hit rock bottom, trying to live someone else's dream, that it became crystal clear. My own life's purpose was to feel good, and I learnt that if I was doing a job that didn't make me feel good, then I needed to change it. If I wasn't living my true passion because fear was holding me back, then I needed to become bigger than my fear.

I had lost touch within my true, inner self along the way because I was busy trying to make everyone else happy. I was trying to fit in with society and do all the right things that were expected of me. At the time, that involved leaving a small country town, getting a great office job, and climbing the corporate ladder. It was the time in my life when I was rewarded for working hard, buying a house, and then being an investor and having another rental property. It didn't matter how much I tried to keep up with society's expectations and the status of success. I soon discovered I wasn't living my own passion and dreams by working in a corporate office, sitting in a confined cubicle, and not being allowed to talk to anyone because we had to work. That was not my thing, and neither was being under constant financial pressure in order to merely obtain social status. I soon discovered that even though I was doing my best to keep up with the repayments of two very large mortgages, none of it was making me happy.

My life has changed so much, and I find more happiness through visiting luxury day spas and writing about them, as well as travelling, meeting amazing people, and finding out more about treatments. I enjoy practicing yoga, meditating, and going for a walk; they are more rewarding than the corporate ladder I was trying to climb. I learnt that even if

I climbed the corporate ladder, it didn't make me happy. It might make other people happy, but you have to come back to yourself and how you feel within.

Make time to tune in to how you are feeling. Be brave, accept, and surrender when something isn't serving your highest good. Sometimes it takes something going completely pear-shaped in your life for you to make the change.

At first you might feel like your whole world is falling apart, but have faith and self-belief. Remember that it is the universe's way to guiding you back to your path. I have had so many redirections throughout my life, and at first I used to take the blows really hard.

I had never experienced being made redundant before, a failed marriage, and so many other things. At the time, I took everything personally. I am only human and still have feelings, and they do get hurt.

I think sometimes we need to go through these unplanned, out-of-control times and experiences in order to personally grow. I truly believe it makes us better people. It helps make things a lot clearer, and it redirects us to the right path.

When I lost my administration job, one of the tasks I had to do was write down all of the things I liked to do. I wrote about writing, talking, spa travel, luxury day spas, skincare, wellness, and health. Not once on the list did I write administration or working in an office. At the time, losing my job felt like the most horrible thing to ever happen, and I was so stressed about how I was going to pay for anything. However, it helped me get clear on what I did love to do, and I ended up pursing what I loved instead of being stuck doing a job that I didn't like and that didn't make me feel good.

I noticed the biggest transformation in my health when I started to do the things I loved. The transformation it makes is amazing when you wake up each day knowing you are going to be doing the things you like.

I am not going to pretend that it happens easily. Like anything, living your life passion and dream doesn't happen overnight. However, accepting that things really do happen for a reason, along with self-belief, is one of the most powerful spiritual lessons I have encountered. I want to share with you just how important self-belief is, along with aligning each day with your truth.

Doing things that make you feel good every day is key. If you want to live a healthy, happy, spiritual life, then you need to be doing things every day that make you feel good. Even if you are a busy professional, mother, business owner, or blogger, it's key that you find time each day to do at least one thing that makes you feel good from within. You need to find your thing, live your passion, and feel good from within. I believe everything starts from within, and when you do things you truly love that come from your own authentic spirit, when you align with your truth, you will become your happiest, healthiest self.

HOW TO GET READY FOR YOUR TWENTY-ONE DAYS OF HAPPY, HEALTHY JOURNEY

Before you start your twenty-one days to wellness, I think it's important to take a little time to get mentally, physically, emotionally, and spiritually prepared. Here are some things worth considering before you start day one of your journey.

- A professional medical doctor's check-up before starting to exercise, to make sure you have the all-clear.
- A BPA water bottle, so you can fill it up with water and carry it everywhere.
- A good pair of walking shoes and trainers that are suitable for working out.
- A yoga mat.
- A notepad and pen for writing and journaling.
- Green tea (preferably organic).
- Healthy, fresh fruits and vegetables; choose a variety and lots of different colours.
- Natural skincare (chemical-free products, if you can).
- An open mind about trying new wellness things.
- A awesome playlist to work out to.

Twenty-one-Day Wellness Guide to Your Happiest, Healthiest, Spiritual Self

Day 1 — Set Your Daily Intention

Before you rush out the front door to start your day, I invite you to set your own daily intentions and goals. I truly believe when you make it clear and put it out there, that is what you will work towards manifesting.

When it comes to manifesting the way you want to feel or the life you want to live, it starts with making it very loud and clear how you would like your day to be. If you want to have a beautiful day, then set you intention to be, "Today, I choose to have a beautiful day." Say it out loud and make it clear, because when you put your energy and focus on it, that is what you will be open to giving and receiving.

When it comes to your own health and fitness goals, once again, make it clear: "Today I am going to go for a twenty-minute walk."

When you set your clear intentions and your own personal goals, you put them out there and focus inwards purely on yourself and your health and happiness. You can live a healthy, happy, passionate, feel-good life. All of this comes simply from setting your daily intentions and getting clear on what goals you would like to manifest daily in order to help you towards your health and wellness goal.

Write down what you want to do today. Choose something that is going to make you feel good, healthy, and happy. It might be that today you choose to eat a healthy breakfast, practice a yoga class after work, go to bed early, and listen to feel-good music when working out. Whatever it is, you want to do write it down, set your daily goal, and then make it happen.

If your ultimate goal is weight loss, then you already know eating healthy and exercising is key, along with drinking lots of water and getting plenty of sleep. But break it down. How are you going to exercise today? Are you going to walk, run, swim, cycle, or do a yoga class? Choose how you are going to exercise and write it down. As soon as you set your intention, along with your goal, all you need to do is make it happen. With the universe's positive energy and force behind you, making it happen won't be a problem; all you have to do is simply believe that you can do it.

Each day, you get to choose how you live your life. You get to choose whether you are going to make your dreams happen, whether you are going to reach your own personal goals. You have the power; all you need to do is get clear on what you need to do. Set your intention, write down your daily goal, and make it happen. If something along the way pops up and stops you from getting to your gym class on time, that's okay; find another way to be active. As long as you are setting your intention and trying your very best to manifest your goals and dreams each day, that is all you can ask for. Each day, take time out to be proud that you have personally gone to the effort to put yourself and your own health and happiness before anything else.

If you want to live your best, healthiest, and happiest spiritual life, you need a full tank of positive energy. It does take a lot of energy in this day and age to keep up with all of the demands placed on us. Lacking energy hampers the way we feel and the lives we live. Not having enough energy to do the things we love can also hold us back and make us miss out on opportunities. Feeling healthy, happy, and full of feel-good spiritual energy is key to living our dreams.

If you want to be bursting with positive, feel-good energy, then get in the habit of spending a couple of minutes daily to set your intention and daily goals. I have a notepad on my kitchen table, and I always set my intentions and goals for the day before I walk out my front door.

You get to set the tone of your day. You get to invite what type of energy you would like to call in. You get to choose whether you want to live your passion and dreams, whether you want to feel good. Everything you needs starts from within.

You are the only one who can get clear on how you would like to feel, what you would like your day to be like, and what goal you would like to achieve. Remember that everything you need comes from within; all you have to do is get it out there so you can manifest the life you truly want to live.

If your intention is to have a beautiful, positive, feel-good day, then write that down or say it out aloud. What you think and say is what your day will become. If you want to feel happy and laugh, then write that down and say it out aloud. When you set your daily intentions, you are truly putting it out there, and it's amazing what you can receive.

Get ready to feel what it's like to give and receive. Set your intentions and make it clear how you would like to feel and what you would like to do.

Each day when you wake up, I want you to practice setting your intentions so that you can call into your life what you want to feel and how you want it to be.

I set my intentions daily, and every day is different from the next. Once you become in tune with what you truly need, and once you take time to sit in silence and listen to your inner self, it will guide you.

Day 2 — Create Space Within

Before you rush out your bedroom door, create space within. Sit in a comfortable place or lie down in your bed, and simply be present. Slowly wake up—don't rush.

Don't grab your mobile phone to look at social media. Instead, close your eyes and focus inwards on your breath. Take five big, deep breaths in through your nose and exhale out through your nose. Breathe with ease, and then after your deep breaths, let everything go, including controlling your breath. Let the natural rhythm of your breath rise and fall; tune inwards to the sensation and check in with how you are truly feeling.

When you feel grounded, centred, and ready to take on the day, get dressed and then go ahead.

It's okay to meditate in your pyjamas. Today's daily wellness challenge is to stop for even a couple of minutes and tune inwards. Creating space within is all about allowing yourself to simply be, so you can connect with your higher self and become spiritually present.

If you want to meditate more than a couple of minutes a day, then I invite you to roll out your yoga mat and find a nice, comfortable, easy space so you can guide your attention inwards. Close your eyes, focus on your breath, and feel all of the sensations as your chest rises and falls.

There are so many great ways to meditate. It can be simply listening to your own breath, or it can be guided meditations, which are available for free on YouTube. All you have to do is type in "guided meditation," and you can even narrow it down to how many minutes you want to meditate for, or for whatever emotional need you want to work on. It might be that you have woken up feeling anxious; all you need to do is type in "guided meditation for anxiety," and then a selection will pop up. I am a fan of the guided meditations on YouTube. I find it to be an easy and accessible way to meditate. If you can wear earphones, it is much better because it blocks out background noise, but it depends on what feels most comfortable for you. Once again, everything comes back to how it makes you feel.

When I first started doing guided meditations from YouTube, I fell in love with some of the meditation teachers' relaxing, meditative voices. Other voices didn't resonate or make me feel great for whatever reason. I encourage you to find a mediation teacher whom you truly love, because that will also make it much easier to keep up your daily meditation practice. However, I also encourage you to try lots of different types of meditation and practices so that you can learn from all the different teachers. There are also many meditation apps available, however my all-time favourite is still calm.com. I love the pretty background pictures, the natural sounds of the ocean, the fireplace, and their mindfulness meditation, which is a full-body scan.

I used to think that in order to be good at meditating, I had to have a clear mind with not one single thought running through my head, like a Buddhist Zen master who had trained years for years doing this meditating for hours or for the whole day.

Of course, I later discovered this thought was not real. When you meditate, it is only natural that your thoughts are going to rise and fall along with your emotions. I discovered that meditation was more to do with guiding my attention back inwards and becoming fully present in the moment by closing my eyes, listening to my breath, and breathing. I could breathe either through my nose and out through my nose, or in through my nose and out through my mouth; there was no right or wrong way when it came to meditating.

It didn't matter whether I was sitting on my yoga mat or in my lounge chair, or on public transports, or on a plane. I could meditate wherever I liked. Again, you don't have to have a dedicated meditation spot. However, if you do decide to create a space at your home to meditate, that is great. When I have a lot more time on the weekends to myself, I love to do much longer meditation practices.

I have found mediating to be as beneficial and as relaxing as going to the day spa, or even going on a holiday. I have found that with regular practice, the health and wellness benefits are amazing. Even after ten or fifteen minutes of doing a meditation for deep relaxation, I open my eyes at the end and feel like I have been on a mini holiday. When I started meditating, my whole life transformed. I was able to better cope with stress, I started to eat better, I slept better, and I felt better. I truly became a happier, healthier, spiritual person from within.

Mediation has transformed my own life, and that's why I now want to share this daily spiritual wellness practice with you. I invite you now to create space and meditate so you can feel good too.

I am not going to tell you that it is easy to wake up every day and create this brand-new habit. It will take some focus, dedication, and work. But once you get the hang of meditating and it becomes part of your day-to-day life, you'll feel better from the inside out and can live your dreams.

I truly believe meditation is the key to feeling good and manifesting anything. It's a beautiful way to start the day. If you have ever wanted to feel more spiritual, this is one of the simplest ways to do so. By focusing on your breath and letting your chest and thoughts rise and fall, you are connecting to your higher self. When you first give this a go, you might not feel like it's doing a lot, but give it time. Practice closing your eyes and focusing on your breath, and over time you will see how this simple technique of meditative breathing can transform so many areas of your life.

Now that you know how to meditate and why I love to meditate, I also want to share with you another daily practice that you can try: being mindful.

If you feel like your mind is taking you back to the past or forward to an uncertain future, creating anxiety around the unknown, then you can do this simple technique of mindfulness. Mindfulness means becoming fully present. When making a cup of tea, it involves becoming aware when you're pouring the hot water from the jug over your tea bag, and watching the steam rise and the waterfall.

Become fully present of what is in front of you, as well as what is happening right now in the present world. Your past or the uncertainty of your future does not exist. All you have is that mindful, present moment, which will give you the much-needed break if you are suffering from depression or anxiety. Practice your mindfulness throughout the day. Become aware of what is right in front of you, along with every action you are doing; observe what is going on around you and within you; take note all the wonderful sensations, colours, sights, smells, and sounds of the world.

You will find that when practicing your mindfulness, like making a cup of tea or dinner, your mind and thoughts might take you away from the present moment. The next thing you are thinking is, "I need to do this or that. I have to put a load of washing on. Oh, I forgot I need to pay that bill yesterday." You may find that your mind is away and out of your body. Your body and spirit may be present, but your mind is out wandering around.

To fully reconnect and become whole again, draw your attention and guide it back inwards to what you are doing at that present moment. A lot of anxiety can rise from our minds time-travelling towards the future. We live in a society that rewards us for always being one step ahead of the game, for always doing that future planning. This is the way we have been taught: we need to be to be successful at the job we do, or at being a mother. However, through this daily habit, we constantly take away from the now, and we can become disconnected within ourselves. Always come back to the now and focus your attention inwards, to what is happening right here and right now.

It's important to recognize that every future thought may or may not happen. You might think that you need to be at an appointment at a certain time, but then you get stuck at work or in traffic. When you go throughout your day being mindful of the present, you can accept whatever doesn't go to plan. You can go with ease and know within that it's okay, that these things happen, so don't stress about them.

Go throughout your day being fully present and mindful of your thoughts. Let them rise and fall, and remember that not every thought is true. Only choose the thoughts that serve your highest good. Be mindful of the words you say about yourself and everyone else. Be mindful of the things you are doing, whether that be driving or paying for your cup of coffee.

Be mindful of what you see in the mirror. Become aware of who you are and how you are. Send yourself loving thoughts, and repeat to yourself while looking in the mirror, "I love you, I love you. I thank you, I thank you." Love what you see, and don't ever beat yourself up or hate yourself. Become your true, loving soul friend.

Day 3 — Nourish Yourself from the Inside Out

Choose to eat healthy, fresh fruits and vegetables. Choose to eat a variety of different types, selecting different colours. Eat a fruit or vegetable salad, and choose the colours of a rainbow. As an example, choose a green apple for green, a watermelon for red, spinach for green, and tomatoes for red. You want to eat a range of different coloured fruits and vegetables because each colour offers different vitamins and nutrients. Mix up your fruits and vegetables each day, and nourish yourself from within.

I am not suggesting that all you are allowed to eat is fresh fruits and vegetables. Instead, I am inviting you to aim to eat the suggested recommendation of five servings of vegetables and two servings of fruit per day. Choose to eat the colours of the rainbow so that you get a variety of vitamins and nutrients. It's a pretty basic concept, and I am sure you hear it all the time, but I believe it's important if you want to live your best, healthiest, happiest spiritual life.

Sometimes we can go through our day without eating a piece of fruit, because we have filled up on processed foods. When we do that, it means we miss out on nourishing ourselves through fresh fruits and vegetables that have grown from the life force of Mother Earth.

There is no better way to be a healthy, happy, down-to-earth wellness girl than through eating fresh, unprocessed fruits and vegetables that were grown from the earth.

When you eat fresh fruits and vegetables, it is coming from a plant-based, earthly source. Try to eat organic if you can. If that is not available or is too expensive, then think of other ways to make eating fresh fruits and vegetables as part of your everyday life.

If buying a fruit salad in a cup works out to be cheaper and more convenient because you live on your own, that is okay. The whole point is to find a way to nourish yourself through eating lots of fresh fruits and vegetables.

If you have gone off eating fresh fruit because you read articles that talked about how much sugar they have, then forget about that. I truly believe that eating fresh fruits and vegetables does wonders for your skin. A lot of people ask me what my skincare tips are, and I always say lots of fresh berries. I believe that because I try my best to eat a lot of fresh fruits and vegetables daily, along with many other wellness things.

If you are reading this and are not feeling healthy and happy, and if you want to have glowing skin, I invite you to eat different coloured fruits and vegetables daily. In time, you will feel and see the different. It truly is an amazing feeling. If you are lacking in energy or are not feeling your positive self, I have found that as soon as I start to eat fresh food that has been grown from Mother Earth, the natural, plant-based life force makes me feel so much better no matter what.

Try today to eat some of your all-time favourite fruits and vegetables. My favourite fruit are raspberries, and my favourite vegetable is sweet potato. When you change the way you feel, it's all about finding fresh fruits and vegetables that you love to eat. When you love something, it is much easier for it to become a part of your daily life. I invite you to try lots of different types of fruits and vegetables. Figure out what you love most and what you don't like. Then choose to eat more of the fresh fruits and vegetables you love, because you are better off eating what you love and nourishing yourself inside and out, as compared to not eating any fruits and vegetables.

If you have a farmers' market that you can go to, you are very blessed indeed. Take the time to walk around and enjoy the experience of selecting fresh, unprocessed fruits and vegetables; it is going to make you feel happy and healthy within. Try to make yourself a smoothie or juice at home, or a nourishing and colourful salad; mix all your colours. Try to have your vegetables raw, in a juice, as a smoothie, in a salad, steamed, baked—you name it. You can do anything when you nourish yourself from the inside and eat the colours of the rainbow. Bring colour into your life with fresh, healthy foods. It will give you some of the nutrients and vitamins you need. It will fill you up and make you feel good within. Explore this today and every waking day throughout the Wellness It Girl program, and beyond.

I was lucky that my mum was so big on eating fresh fruit every day. I remember her sitting down for afternoon tea and having a piece of fresh fruit, whether it was an apple, nectarine, or orange. I love that she still reminds me to this very day how important fresh fruit is.

Sometimes we can tell ourselves that eating fresh fruit doesn't fill us up, or that eating a salad doesn't fill us up. Then we might turn to something like a sandwich with butter and a spread, or crackers and cheese, or a yoghurt. Before we know it, we haven't had any fruit during the day.

Once you create a daily habit of eating fresh fruits and vegetables, the more you do it, the more you will crave it. You might not think you will after one day of eating lots of fresh fruits and vegetables, but give it time, and you definitely will.

Day 4 — Become a Green Tea or Tea Goddess

Be a green tea or tea goddess. You may have tried a cup of green tea in the past and not liked it. however when you find the right quality green tea and put a little water on your tea bag first, it can make drinking a cup of tea much more pleasurable. It's about discovering a quality green tea you love drinking. You may have tried buying green tea from the supermarket and discovered you hated the taste of it. Drink quality green tea so that it's enjoyable and tastes good, and so you can receive the full health and antioxidant benefits.

Green tea is full of antioxidants. It's great for stress, weight loss, health, wellness, and your skin. I have found the best green tea off the shelf in the Australian supermarket to be Madame Flavour delicate green jasmine and pear. Even though it might be coming off the shelf at the supermarket, I have found this brand to be the best and the most drinkable. I was introduced to this green tea from one of my adorable Spa It Boys, believe it or not. He gave me this insider tip, and at first I was unsure, as a wellness blogger, whether I was going to like green tea that was bought from the supermarket. I tried this brand and really loved it.

You can go to your local teashop and ask for a green tea that they think would be the best. It might be your first time drinking a cup of green tea, so try a few in store to make sure before you buy. If you are coming back after an experience when you drank a poor cup of green tea, then I think it's important to find a nice brand you like drinking.

If you try it and still don't feel that drinking green tea is for you, that's okay. Become a general tea goddess instead. Drinking almost any tea will still give you the benefits and antioxidants. In the afternoon, if you are still looking for a little caffeine hit, it will give you a little, but it if you're sensitive to caffeine or already feeling stressed, it won't make you feel more stressed. Rather, you'll feel relaxed and calm instead.

Day 5 — Be a Natural Beauty

Choose natural skincare products that have no chemicals in them and are not tested on animals. You can use organic products, or natural, chemical-free products, on your skin. Being a natural beauty is all about reducing the chemicals and toxins on your skin, because your skin, especially around your face, penetrates in. Be mindful to choose skincare products that are chemical free. Choose chemical-free, natural products that will do wonders for your skin, health, and well-being. Try different natural skincare products until you find a brand you love and that you feel works for you. Some of my favourite Australian brands for chemical free natural skincare I truly love using Australian, chemical-free, vegan, natural skincare products on my skin. Australia has so many amazing natural skincare products, but it's all about finding what works best for your skin when it comes to your own skincare routine.

Choose natural skincare products that are based on natural ingredients and are not tested on animals so that you are reducing the direct chemicals you are putting on your skin.

My aunty has always been big on using natural skincare products, and she is a big believer that the products you put on your skin are what penetrate into your system. I have to agree, and that's why I also love using natural skincare: I know that

I am not putting harmful chemicals directly on my face and skin. I try my best to always use natural skincare products when I can, because our skin is the largest organ, and whatever we put on it easily absorbs into our system. I like to go for chemical-free products so I can reduce the amount of harmful toxins I am putting on my skin and that go into my own system.

I just spent some time in Hong Kong and visited a retail organic and spa store called Beyorg. It was so refreshing to see how many organic skincare brands from around the world they had available in their store. None of the products had been tested on animals, and that was very cool because I am an animal lover, so naturally I love any store or spa that has an organic, not-animal-tested option.

I invite you to find a natural skincare brand that you personally love. Then follow this basic natural skincare beauty daily routine, morning and night.

- Cleanse
- Exfoliate (or tone)
- Moisturise your face with face cream, and moisturize under the eyes with eye cream
- Add into your routine an anti-ageing serum to pop under or over your face moisturizer

Once a week, pop on a facemask, either a hydrating one if your skin is feeling dehydrated, or a deep-cleansing mask if you want to unclog your pores. Tune into what your skin needs to choose the best mask for you. If you are unsure what your skin type is or what is happening within your skin, then have a facial and let your trained beauty therapist or spa therapist assist you.

Never wear make-up when working out, and always go to bed with a clean face that's not covered in make-up. These simple daily tips will let your skin breathe and will help prevent your pores clogging up.

A lot of people ask me for my skincare tips, and I respond with the fact that I only like to use natural skincare products. I also don't like to wear a lot of make-up, and I have always focused more my day-to-day skincare and cleaning my skin. Using natural, organic skincare products has done wonders for my skin.

When it comes to natural skincare beauty, I also think the number one anti-aging skincare product is sunscreen. The more you can protect your skin from the harmful sun, the better. It will help slow down the aging process and prevent any sun damage to your skin.

I had a work friend who had to get some skin cancer cut out from her face. She shared with me what a horrible feeling it was; she has never had a scar on her face before, but now she does. She is having to overcome this major change to her and is now the biggest ambassador to encouraging everyone to wear sunscreen on the face. She has spent years travelling around on the road as a sales representative, and living in Australia, which has such high UV rays, has damaged her skin. I have to agree that wearing sunscreen daily is key.

A lot of people don't like to wear sunscreen because it might wear off, run into their eyes, and sting. I think it's important to find a sunscreen—and a natural one, if possible—that you can wear each day and that doesn't run into your eyes, sting, or make your skin feel horrible and sticky.

Day 6 — I Like to Move It, Move It

Make the time to move it, to exercise. It makes you feel good. That is why I have always loved exercising: because whether or not I had money, it didn't matter. I could always go outside, exercise, and feel great. I found exercise from a very young age, and it always made me feel good. When I connected with feeling good, I learnt that was why I wanted to exercise.

As you get older, along the way your reasoning for exercise might change, and you might change your mindset. "I need to exercise to lose weight." However, I invite you to focus on the reason you need to exercise is so you can feel good. It's amazing what a difference changing your reason can make. I personally believe that sometimes we are too hard on ourselves; I know this from my own personal experience. Even I found myself stressing myself out at times, and there would be days when I felt completely buggered from either overtraining or over-working. I would still tell myself, *I have to go exercise to lose weight.* It had nothing at times to do with feeling great.

I now believe it's important to exercise in order to feel great, and to also tune in to how you are feeling. If your inner self is guiding you to take a low-impact walk, then do that. If you are being guided to go for a run because you are bursting with energy, then do that. Tune into what you need when you exercise to feel good. No matter what kind of day you have, you always know you can feel good through exercise, which is much better than sitting down and drinking a bottle of wine by yourself.

When you choose to exercise, it will get your own feel-good endorphins pumping through your body, mind, and spirit. It will make you feel good, especially at the end, after you have worked out.

If you have been feeling low and don't feel like you have the energy to exercise, then go for a gentle walk. Even if it's to your mailbox and back, it might be only a couple of minutes, and that's a start. When it comes to exercising, it has to start from within and your willingness to want to feel better. Exercising is so powerful when it comes to making you feel better, so simply focus on how it is the best thing for your health and wellness. Shifting your mindset to how amazing it is going to make you feel will help you get over that hurdle of "I know I should be exercising, but I can't be bothered" feeling.

Gentle exercise is a great way to lift your spirit and improve your mood. If you are feeling a little down, then go for a nice walk amongst nature to lift your heart and soul. Exercising and "moving it" mean different things for different people. You might love going for a walk, a bike, ride, or a swim.

For me, I love moving it and exercising by practicing yoga, going for walks amongst nature, and then going to the gym and doing a full-on, high-energy Les Mills body attack class with others in a fun, upbeat-music, fitness environment. This is my go-to class because it's so much fun. Yes, it is hard and really gets your heart rate up. When I was twenty-five kilos heavier and not my healthiest and happiest self, I started doing Les Mills body attack classes, and I started in the back row. I was always used to being on the front stage, so you imagine how I was feeling. But because I felt so unfit, being in the back row allowed me to get over the feeling of "I don't want anyone else to see how unfit I am." In time, by doing more and more Les Mills body attack classes, I clawed my way back up to the front row. Now I encourage other girls and women to do the same.

I personally think I am now a better fitness and wellness professional, qualified aerobics teacher, and personal trainer after having personally experienced what it was like to hit rock bottom and put on so much weight. Before that, I had always had a good metabolic rate, and I had never personally experienced what it was like to be overweight and the struggle that went with that. It was the first time in my life that I truly experienced what it was like to struggle to tie my own shoes, and how it was so hard to try do even do a sit-up because so much of my weight was sitting on my stomach, which the doctor told me was one of the riskiest places to store weight. I now believe I am a much more understanding health, wellness, and fitness professional.

I am not going to sugar-coat it: it wasn't easy, and especially when you are struggling in the class, and all of a sudden someone scoots past and don't even look like she is breaking out in a sweat. I want you to know that you have the power to change the way you feel. Exercising and moving it makes you feel good (after the workout), and that is a key lifestyle ritual that is going to make you become your happiest and healthiest self.

The key is finding a way to move it that makes you feel good and that will keep you coming back for more. Aim to exercise at least three times a week for thirty minutes. However, if you can exercise five times a week, that's even better. Find what suits you best and base it around what you want to achieve from your workouts.

If you are trying to lose weight, the first thing you need to do when you are moving it is to stop thinking about how you are exercising to lose weight. When you exercise purely to have fun, to feel good, and to get the endorphins going, you will move more thoroughly through your weight-loss challenge. You need not stress out about it, because the less you stress, the quicker you can become happier and calm. That is when you let go of that unwanted weight and emotional baggage, stress, and tension that you have been holding and that has been preventing you from losing the weight.

I also recommended doing resistance training a couple of times a week. Mix up your workouts with one day of cardio then the next day resistance training. If doing weights at the gym isn't your thing, there are plenty of other ways to work on your resistance training: yoga, reformer Pilates, high-intensity interval training, and more. If you have never done weights before but have always wanted to try it, then I recommend finding a suitable personal trainer, because you always want to make sure you are doing your resistance training in a safe, controlled environment. The most important thing is technique.

My apartment is one active living space. As a Les Mills body pump teacher, it's rather funny because I have two Reebok body pump bars in my laundry. Then near my TV I have Reebok weights for the body pump bars. I have a foam roller, which I use to roll out my back when I need to, plus little hand dumbbells. I even have a hula hoop (which my nieces love to use when they visit). I've got weight bands to put on my ankles and a skipping rope. In my cupboard, I have all of my old aerobics workout cassettes that I couldn't part with, plus of course loads of Les Mills DVDs and CDs. For some time now, I've been collecting different yoga DVDs, plus

I have loads of Tracy Anderson Workout DVDs. I've even got a belly dancing workout DVD, and a Zumba workout DVD. When I chose my apartment, I wanted to be able to move my blogger's couch, as I like to call it, out of the way so I could transform my living room into my workout studio. It's been great because I am such a big fan of making your place into an active living space. I have found this to be great when I miss a class or the gym, or when it's raining outside and is not ideal to go out for a walk.

If you can't afford to join the gym, that's okay because there are loads of workouts you can do on YouTube, or you can pick up a workout DVD and do it at home. You can buy yourself a hula hoop and try that. I grew up with my mum exercising at home, and this has rubbed off on me. She used to skip everyday when I was in primary school, and I remember her always counting up to five hundred skips a day. Then as I entered high school, we started buying workout videos. My brother had all of the Billy Banks tae-bo, and that was a great workout. I grew up in a place that didn't have any guys at the time, so it was the most exciting thing when workout videos starting coming out, and the person was from America or another country. I thought, *Wow!*

I remember the first workout video I bought was the Claudia Schiffer workout video. I must admit at the time, because I was so young, I thought if I did the workout enough times,

I would get long, lanky legs like her. I now know that no matter how much you work out, you will never look like anyone other than yourself. We all have different shapes and sizes. Sure, we all have the ability to get fit and healthy, but it doesn't mean if you do a personal trainer class, you are going to look like them. You are always going to look like you, so embrace who you are and work out so you can become the best version of yourself.

Day 7 — Self-love Sunday

One of the best gifts you could ever give to yourself is self-love. If you want to live your happiest, healthiest, spiritual life, you must first love yourself.

When we think about love, we may believe that in order to feel loved, it must come from someone else. Then we think if we do not have that someone else, we are not loved.

One of the things I have learnt along my spiritual journey is that in ordered to feel loved and to love, it has to come from within. Through practicing self-love on a Sunday (and every other waking day), that is how you feel love.

It's great to receive love from someone else, however when that love is gone, it can leave you feeling like you are no longer loved anymore. That can have you searching for love in all the wrong places, just so you can feel love.

Whether or not you are in a relationship, it really doesn't matter. Self-love is all about loving yourself from within, and it's about having a happy, healthy, loving relationship with yourself so that no matter where you are on Mother Earth, you are your best loving girlfriend.

When you make the time to connect to your higher spirit and self, you will experience self-love. The reason is that each and every one of us is a loving spiritual being. We might not always feel like it because we have latched onto overly obsessive thoughts, and we might be in a pattern of self-hate and self-destructive, negative thoughts.

I personally struggled for a long time to make peace with myself from within. I cultivated my self-love Spa It Girl lifestyle, which is all about loving yourself for who you are, as you are. It involves loving yourself through kind, loving, nurturing things like exercising, healthy eating, visiting day spas, practicing yoga, meditating, and practicing every single self-love Sunday, which I will explain in greater detail. I was able to turn about the feelings that I wasn't good enough, or that I didn't have the perfect body.

My self-love struggles started early on in my early teenager years, when I really wanted to travel the world visiting different places as a model at the time growing up in a small town I discovered that was one way to discover the world. I didn't realize at the time when I was starting out that being a size ten and a natural size 10DD would mean I would get selected for the jobs and all I received was a constant knock back of "Sorry, you are not what we are looking for." For catwalk or fashion photography modelling, they needed a very slim, straight, up-and-down shape. I was often told I was too big and needed a flat chest. I needed to drop a full dress size, and when I did come back then, I was told by one guy that I was carrying too much weight to become a model; the only ones who made it were super skinny. Of course, I soon discovered I was never going to fit into the mainstream media because I had curves. I remember turning up to one casting and seeing this very slim, stick-like, no-curves model eating salads. When tried that, it didn't work for me; I felt hungry and sick. There were even lots of girls purging and doing all sorts of unhealthy things, and it wasn't a great thing. Sometimes in mainstream media, they show the unhealthy sides of the real fashion modelling industry.

I decided to no longer try being something I was not. I also decided it was much healthier to eat, exercise, work out, and be happy. Not smiling and having a serious face wasn't for me either. You only have to look at my Instagram account (@spaitgirl) to realize that no matter how hard I try, I was born to smile.

It took a long time to make peace with myself, because even when I was in grade seven, I was developing very quickly to a DD cup. I remember one day when I was finishing primary school, and it was my first time wearing a bra underneath my school top. When I went to get my bike off the rack, one of the boys from my class yelled so everyone could hear, "Yvette's wearing a bra!" I felt so embarrassed, humiliated, and ashamed. Developing was a new thing for me, and at the time, I think I was unsure of what was going on with my own body. I lived in a small town, which was renowned for people always talking about others. I got so upset, started crying, and ran off. I threw my bike on the ground, and then that same kid started jumping on my front tyre, buckling it. I waited till everyone rode off on their bikes, and then I went to get my bike, not realizing that I couldn't ride it. I had to push my bike home and felt very down.

From that moment onwards, I developed an unhealthy relationship with my body. When I went on to high school, I wore a big, baggy top. I even rounded my shoulders instead of standing tall and confident—all to hide that I had bigger natural 10DD boobs when everyone else around me had A or B cups. Of course, it's a different story today, because so many girls would love to have a natural 10DD cup, and in social media having bigger breasts even sometimes gets all the likes and followers. However, when I started out online blogging, it was for the love of my own passions and my love of making others feel good within, so I never wanted to have people like me or know me just for my boobs. I wanted people to love me for who I was as a person and for my own kind and authentic spirit.

I think that is why I love being a spa wellness lifestyle blogger so much, as well as the founder of Spa It Girl. It doesn't matter what shape, size, or fitness level you are, or what you look like. It's all about feeling good. Every other Spa It Girl I see hanging out and relaxing in a dreamy bathtub, or rocking it in a bathrobe, is always glowing with self-love and happiness. To me, that is always what I wanted to create through Spa It Girl: a global community that was all about feeling good from the inside out. It had nothing to do with body image, looking sexy and hot, six-pack abs, or big boobs. I wanted to empower girls around the world to love themselves and to always choose self-love over self-hate, even when they are trying to reach their own personal weight-loss goals or any goal.

I believe self-love is all about accepting and loving yourself for who you are as you are. It's about choosing kind, loving thoughts towards yourself and choosing to love yourself from the inside out, unconditionally and no matter what your body shape or size is. I understand that sometimes when we feel like we have let ourselves go and are not feeling our happiest and healthiest, we can look in the mirror and say, "I wish I had a tight bum, six-pack abs, and a thinner waist." But by wishing and not being happy with what you see, you end up taking yourself away from your true, authentic self and your higher spirit. In order to be present and connected from within, you have to love yourself as you are. There is no wishing required, because right now, all you need to do is love yourself.

When you practice self-love, it helps change the way you feel. Instead of getting caught up in negative thoughts about how much you hate yourself, or the things that you hate about yourself, it teaches you to accept the way you are and to love yourself for who you are, how you are right now.

One of the greatest ways you can practice self-love is through a beautiful, gentle yoga practice. I found yoga to be the turning point in my life. When I came to terms with who I was and how I was, I found a place of self-acceptance and self-love. By practicing yoga regularly, I am much happier within myself and about myself. I now know it's okay to have curves or to be the shape I am, because that is who I am. But before I started practicing yoga, it was a very different story because when I was growing up as a teenager, I wanted to get into modelling in order to travel the world. No matter how many times I tried, it wasn't meant to be. The only thing I remember from that experience was being told on so many occasions that I needed to have a flat chest and be a lot smaller. After all of these experiences, I started to question my body image. I couldn't understand why I didn't fit in. Then I started to think it was because I was a size ten with a natural 10DD chest.

As I grew older and wiser, I started to realise that it was actually the media who was controlling what we should all like and it was because of the magazines we saw or the people on TV we saw that we were led to believe only those who are skinny or a certain body shape were worthy to be represented in the media. I then discovered this wasn't true and the real picture should be one that showed all different shapes and sizes and looks; by doing that, every girl would feel good about herself because the media was showing the real picture, and not one girl would feel she didn't fit in or was too fat to be on the cover of a magazine.

After my own personal modelling experience. I became a group fitness instructor. I realized it didn't matter what size I was; as long as I was fit and healthy and could inspire and motivate others to exercise and feel good, that was all that mattered. My own personal body image experiences also made me become very passionate about self-love, and I developed a strong empowering message to other girls that if you are not on the front cover of a magazine, you are still beautiful, so believe it.

Over the many years, my frustration seemed to grow because no one wanted to show off curvy, size-ten girls. However, with online social media being so big these days, this has changed. Every girl, no matter the shape, size, or what she looks like, can express herself. You only have to look at Instagram to see all the different girls' shapes and sizes, and it's a positive for body image.

I still believe that self-love has to come from within. For so many of us, we have our own stories growing up; even to this day, we may feel like we might not fit in or be considered good enough to be featured in a society obsessed with media. I am here to tell you regardless of your past experiences, today is the turning point for you. Start working every Sunday (and hopefully every other day) on loving yourself the way you are right now. As you read this book, know that you are good enough, you are enough, you are beautiful, you are amazing, you are worthy of love, and you are love. Now is the time to surrender to anything that doesn't serve your highest good. Now is the time to make peace with your stomach or thighs, if that has what has been holding you back from loving yourself. Now is the day that you accept and love yourself just the way you are.

Expressing love and feeling love towards yourself and within can be one of your biggest challenges. I know that especially for someone who is constantly in the public eye, it can be easy to compare yourself to not just the girl on the cover of the magazine but with hundreds of thousands of social media profiles. From my own personal experience, I know that comparing yourself with others will only make you feel sick within; it will bring your mood down and will send self-destructive, negative energy and thoughts to you, especially if you are looking at a bikini blogger and wishing you had a body like hers.

One of the best ways to stop comparing yourself with others is to want to be like yourself and nobody else. When you start working on increasing your self-love, it's a bit like weight training or working out. You will get stronger, and before long you will be able to proudly stand in front of the mirror.

When it comes to self-love, it's important to recognize that there are some things we can't change. As an example, take my height. Even if I wanted to be 180 centimetres tall, I am only 172 centimetres tall, and that is the way it is. It's important to know that in order to love myself, I have to accept and love that I am this height. No matter how much I try to beat myself up put myself down, wishing I was the height of Elle McPherson, the reality is I am 172 centimetres. I now have to make a choice: do I love myself for who I am, or do I spend the rest of my life at war with myself and beating myself up from the inside, which is only going to affect the way I feel? Plus, long term it's going to cause unnecessary stress that can manifest as me living an unhappy life, hating myself, or getting sick. Stress is not good for anyone's health.

I used my height as an example, but you might be able to think of a body part you just don't like or outright hate. I invite you to get a pen and paper and write down everything that you hate when it comes to yourself. I want you to then write down beside each one why. Is it because of something someone said to you whilst growing up? Is it because you have been comparing yourself to fitness models? Is it because you want to be like the girl on the cover of a magazine? What is your reasoning for why you hate yourself?

It's important to know that one size does not fit all, and that everyone is different. It's liberating when you make a change with your thought pattern and connect with the fact that you don't have to be like anyone else. When you fully connect with your true, authentic self, it is a very liberating feeling. Another amazing thing is that when you love yourself for who you are, the chances are high that you will start to love and accept all people for who they are. No one is perfect, and there is no ideal, perfect body shape. All there are on Mother Earth are unique different individuals, spiritual beings. When we focus on being our authentic, spiritual selves, we no longer have to struggle with ourselves.

When you choose to become aware that you are a spiritual being and not just a physical being, you will soon discover that you are enough as you are, and that everything is about feeling happy, healthy, and spiritual from the inside. It's also about being kind, caring, loving, and spiritually aware of others. It has nothing to do with your dress size, shape, or size.

For women, this can be our greatest obstacle to overcome. We have always seen beauty talked about or portrayed in certain ways. In order to be beautiful, society says, you must look like a certain type. Once you grasp that being beautiful is all about your kind, caring, compassionate, spiritual being and heart, your whole perspective changes, and you will be able to spiritually pick up on positive, spiritual, beautiful, radiating energy. Before too long, you won't be focusing on what someone else looks like. You will focus on how someone makes you feel, and how you make yourself feel.

Self-love can be a constant challenge, but that's okay. I know you can overcome it. Try to help with strengthening your own inner self-love. Try this little exercise.

List everything you love about yourself. Then write the list of everything you hate about yourself. If you can't think of one thing, then you definitely are practicing self-love in the most magnificent way. However, if you can think of one or more things, don't beat yourself up right now. Simply write it down.

When it comes to the list of things you hate about yourself, write down why. Where did this come through? Is a thought that came from within? Is it from the past, and you now need to heal it? Is it from something you heard or said?

Take a look at the two lists to see the balance. Do you have more in the self-love list, or more in the self-hate list? Now is your time to choose one of the things from your self-hate list and work on changing that negative thought. Send it some love. The next time you sit down and look at the things you love about yourself and hate about yourself, it moves from your self-hate list to your self-love list. One by one, you are going to break down the self-hate list that is not coming from your highest truth. Your self-hate list is not coming from your true inner self and loving being; it is comprised of energy and thoughts that do not serve your highest good. If you want to be your healthiest and happiest self, you are going to have to actively work on self-love.

Once you get rid of that self-hate, you will soon recognize that no thoughts of hate towards you come from your inner loving self. You have so many thoughts, and quite often the mind naturally wants to give you negative self-talk. Even when you work out, meditate, or practice yoga, you are still going to find times when you are having self-hate, negative, self-destructive thoughts. It's important to recognize that none of these thoughts can hurt you. Not every thought is true, and not every thought comes from your truth. Whenever you find yourself having an inner dialogue, and your thoughts try to bring you down, send your thoughts and yourself some love. When you do, your inner spirit and the universe will always guide you.

Choose to love you for you. Never choose to beat yourself up or to self-hate. You are the most beautiful spiritual being, so embrace your true, inner, authentic, loving self. Everything is okay, and you are safe. You don't need to change anything in order to feel you are enough or are complete. You are already enough.

Every time you catch yourself looking in a mirror and automatically releasing a negative, self-hate thought, pause, take a deep breath, and remember that the thought is not true. Your higher self comes only from a place of love. Say your mantra, which could be something as simple as "I love my thighs, because that is who I am." Then you can smile and say, "Take that, self-hate!" Because a thought pops up, that does not mean it's true. Choose to love yourself unconditionally. When you start loving yourself from within, your whole world is going to change in the most amazing ways.

When you start to love yourself the way you are, you increase the happy, feel-good loving, positive energy. You radiate at a much higher frequency when it comes to connecting to the universe. You also start to surrender to the struggle within that you may have been holding on to for years; you give up your inner secret that you have been holding on to, which you might not have shared with anyone. It's okay to tell people that you have embarked on a self-love Sunday journey. That means every single Sunday, you are going to take time out for yourself to love yourself. It could be having a long, relaxing bath, or buying yourself a bouquet of flowers. It could be getting a haircut, watching a feel-good movie, or writing positive, self-love affirmations about yourself. You can practice a beautiful relaxation, and it's okay to tell people you are making peace from within. I share across the Spa It Girl social media some of the things I am doing on Sundays, and I always invite my readers to join me.

Self-love Sunday started thanks to the amazing, positive influence of my mum, who used to make every Sunday her day of rest and relaxation. She would sit on the front steps and paint her toenails. It was a day of self-love and self-care. As a global spa blogger and founder of the Spa It Girl, I too have made Sunday my self-love Sunday. That is the day I pop on a facemask and do wonderful, kind, loving things to love my body, mind, and soul.

The more you practice self-love towards yourself, the more you will connect with your higher self. I know not everyone gets Sunday off, and that's okay. Sunday is always my designated day, but I think it's important to love yourself every single day, no matter what. We can spend a lot of time worrying about other people, or working on our relationship with someone else. The most important relationship we have to master is the one with ourselves. Once you master loving yourself from within, you will make peace from within, and you no longer have to fight with yourself because all you are going to be doing is giving love and receiving love. It is a much more positive, radiant, loving feeling than hating yourself. I think self-love is one of the most important things that we can master; when we do, it will change the way we feel.

Make time today to love yourself. Practice self-love today by telling yourself how much you love yourself. Throughout the day and night, do things that make you feel loved from within. Start your day with a beautiful, positive affirmation: "I am love." Repeat this affirmation throughout the day to raise the positive vibrations within you. Set your intention for self-love so that you can raise your love and vibrations, and so you can connect with yourself. Imagine yourself as a little kid again, and then close your eyes. Come into a seated position, or you can do this sitting in your chair. We are going to start our self-love Sunday with a guided meditation, mantra, and positive affirmation. Here are the easy-to-follow meditation steps.

Come into a nice, easy place. Sit up in a comfortable, cross-legged position, resting your hands on your knees, or you can lie down on your yoga mat or in a comfortable chair. Take a moment to settle in. Close your eyes. Focus your attention inwards and on your breath. Next, I invite you to ask yourself the question, "Who am I?" See what arises for you. If nothing comes to you when you ask yourself the question, that's okay. I will get you to repeat the question again: "Who am I?"

Then bring your feelings, thoughts, and sensations to the present self-love Sunday moment, and repeat the positive affirmation.

"Who am I? I am love, I am love, and I am love." Repeat the positive affirmation until your inner self guides you to stop. Self-love must come from within, and it's within you. By taking the time out on this Sunday, and every other Sunday, you can cultivate and make the time to actively practice self-love within and towards yourself. All the love you need comes from within. You are a loving being, but sometimes we can get so bogged down in our day-to-day lives that the first thing to go out the window is taking care of ourselves. We can spend so much time worrying about everyone else's needs. Self-love Sunday is a day each week we get to take the time to fully care about ourselves.

I think that generally, every love song is about loving someone else. It's ingrained in our society that it's our duty to love others more than we love ourselves, and that taking time out to love ourselves can be selfish because we are not thinking about everyone else. But we are now thinking about ourselves. If you are feeling unloved from within, it doesn't matter how much love you give to other people— there is always going to be something missing from within and that is the love to yourself. It's already there and already within, but perhaps it has been something you have been ignoring or refusing to believe; perhaps you have had a bad experience when it comes to your own body image, or you have found yourself comparing yourself with others. Maybe it was a partner; in my case, one used to tell me I had a fat arse. When I was in my early twenties, I had such low self-esteem that I believed him. Of course, it was not true; I simply had an arse that was mine, and I was a size ten. It's little things like that, when you are not connected to your higher loving self, that can change the way you feel and the way you see yourself.

Whatever the reasons are, the great news is that through practicing self-love Sunday every week, and then every day, you can overturn and overcome all of the negative thoughts and feelings, and you can make peace from within and give up the inner struggles to realize that you are enough as you are. You are kind, loving, and beautiful, and you are more than your actual body shape. You are a loving, spiritual being, and that beauty is more than just a body shape. Beauty is about how you make others feel, and how you make yourself feel. All the love you need comes from within, and no matter how hard you search to find love and receive it from other people, the most important love you need to give and receive is to and from yourself.

It's an amazing feeling when you connect with your true, inner self, and when you feel the love from your highest self. I remember the first time this happened. Even when it happens to me along my spiritual journey, words cannot describe how amazing it feels to live in harmony with your loving spirit. I now invite you to practice self-love Sunday and to start your day by looking in the mirror and saying,

"I love you, I really do." If you find yourself cringing or wanting to look away, say it out loud again. Get used to being on your own, to expressing love to your higher self, and to receiving it. Keep practicing this until you can stand there confidently and can believe in it.

Also, if you want to join into the Spa It Girl self-love moment, and you are on Instagram or Facebook, be sure to mark any of your self-love Sunday photos with #iamaspaitgirl, and tag @spaitgirl so I can personally see, along with the rest of the global Spa It Girl community, some of the things you are doing on self-love Sunday. That way you can inspire others to take up this all-important healthy, happy, spiritual practice of loving yourself unconditionally no matter what.

Self-love is an absolute must. It can take a bit of practice, but when you start loving yourself more and more every day, it makes you feel so much better from within.

Self-love starts from within.

Day 8 — Monday Morning Gratitude

Create Space Within

It's easy to wake up on Monday and dread having to go to work. Your inner thoughts can sometimes go like this. "I wish I didn't have to go to work. I wish it was still the weekend. I wish I could stay home on the couch and do nothing. I wish the weekend was long." You can get into this negative mindset even before you have gotten out of bed! From those thoughts, you can invite in a guaranteed Monday blue mood.

If you want to feel better on a Monday and raise your happy, feel-good thoughts and energy from within, start today and throughout the whole day to say what you are grateful for. "I am grateful for ..." Whatever it might be, put it out there. Say it out loud and write it down. It could be something as simple as being grateful for your health and wellness, or that you have a job to go to. It's Monday morning, so you get to pick up your morning coffee from your favourite coffee barista. I am often grateful for the sunshine and the blue skies.

Take the time today to count your blessings, to be grateful, and to express gratitude to others. Go throughout the day being grateful. Being grateful will change the way you feel inside, and it will fill you up with lots of positive energy and feel-good vibes. You will get off to a good start for the week, feeling like it's okay. It will also help shift the Monday blues. Create space within, even by trying a little Monday gratitude meditation. Today is the day you truly want to be grateful for everything that is blessed in your life.

Once you start turning your attention to the things that you are grateful for, it also turns your energy and focus to the more positive feelings, energy, and emotions, and it will also help change the way you feel. Today you have the choice to either feel good, and be grateful, and get on with your day through the most beautiful way. Or you can choose to get stuck on that song that keeps playing over in your head, telling you how terrible it is that it's Monday, and how crap things really are by focusing your attention on these negative thoughts and feelings. That approach is going to make you feel like you are having another crappy Monday.

What I love to do on a Monday when I first wake up is create some space. I do a little stretch when I am first waking up in bed, and then I make myself a cuppa and sit on my yoga mat. I am grateful for the little things, like the blue clear skies, the sunshine, and how I have woken up.

Now it's time to set my intentions and daily goals. I am always so grateful that I have a job to go to, because I wouldn't survive without it due to the cost of living. When you look at things through being grateful, it does change the way you feel, and it reminds you about how amazing your life already is. I truly believe nothing lasts forever when it comes to careers, friends, family, situations, times in our lives, our age, and our looks. I love to practice being grateful on Mondays when I find even I need it the most. I am only human, and not having to do anything on the weekend is the best feeling.

I like to practice being grateful every day. Sometimes it might be I am grateful that I even have a car to drive, or a beautiful mum or dad, sisters, brothers, little nieces whom I adore, and beautiful Spa It Girl blog readers. Every day I am grateful is different from the day before or the day ahead. Being grateful is all about being in the present moment and connecting to what you are most grateful for. Though my own personal experience, I do believe that the more you become grateful for, the more it makes you feel good, as well as others. Everyone loves to be appreciated, and I think the nicest thing you can do is express your sincere gratitude when your higher spirit or universe calls for it.

Be grateful today and every single day. When you do so, you are absolutely connecting to your higher self and being a true spiritual being. What you give out is what you get back, and when you come from a place of gratitude, the universe has your back. In my case, from what I have learnt with growing my Spa It Girl blog globally, those whom you are sincerely grateful for will have your back too.

Day 9 — Stretch It Real Good to Feel Good

Today is all about being mindful and taking the time to breathe and stretch, and to release any tension you are holding within. If you will be working within an office today, in front of a computer, I invite you to focus your attention inwards and check in with how you are sitting at your desk. Are you hunched over? Is your back rounded or straight? Are your shoulders rolled up, back, and round?

When sitting down for long periods of time, get up and move around, shake out your body, and then come back to sitting. We can sit down all day in front of the computer and go for hours without moving. However, today is all about combining stretching, focusing on your posture, and having little breaks from sitting down all day.

You can try today's activity if you are sitting in front of a computer all day. Take in a big, deep breath. Take your fingers and hands off the keyboard, resting them on your lap. Just take a moment to breathe and connect to your breath. Take a few shoulder rolls backwards, feeling the sensations happening there. Then take a few shoulder rolls forward.

Tip your head up to the ceiling to stretch out your neck. Then tip your head down, looking towards your chest. You can do that a couple of times. Do a few side-to-side neck stretches, looking towards your left side and then right side. When you turn your neck to one side, it should feel comfortable; you never want to feel any pain in the neck when doing this stretch. You should still be able to breathe with ease. You can then do one of my favourite stretches, which I like to do when sitting in front of the computer for long periods of time. Take your hand to the top of your head and a little way to the side. Then give it a slight neck stretch. Swap opposite hands and sides.

There are so many stretches you can do. You can stretch out through your shoulders and side to side. Then you can interlace your hands and put them in front and then look down. You can open through your chest by taking your hands out and opening your arms wide, so you can feel the stretch right across your chest. You can even do triceps, wrists, and biceps stretches. Tune into what you need to do for yourself.

If you want to go one step further, try a yoga class either at a yoga studio or gym, or through YouTube. Make the time to let go and simply stretch; it's a great way to release the tension and pressure from your day.

Day 10 — You Are a Walking Queen

Go for a walk today, because you are the walking queen. Before you go to work, go for a morning walk, or do it at lunch or after work. I like to mix up my walk pace. If you are brand-new to exercise or are coming back after having some considerable time off, I suggest taking it easy. Go for a flat walk to find your feet. Then over time, build up your distance and speed while walking.

If you have been exercising for some time, then mix up your walks and do a combination of flat walks and hill or stair walks. When I am doing my flat walks, I like to do a fast power walk, where I am pumping my arms. Even though most people walk with their hands down beside them, I find this makes me feel like a penguin. I like to mix it up, and when I am doing a power walk, I will pump my arms to work my arms and my shoulders to get the most out of my walk. Plus, I find it helps to build the intensity, and as an aerobics teacher in a high-intensity class or any aerobics class, all movements I have taught include adding your arms. Doing this results in a greater workout. When you want to drop the intensity, you can put your hands to the side and do a casual walk.

Other things I like to do while walking—and I invite you to give it a go—is to have your favourite upbeat music that gets you into the mood and helps push you along your walk. It can make all the difference if you are finding it hard to get motivated, if you feel like you can't be bothered going for a walk or exercising.

Create your own motivation within by mixing up your walks with some interval training. You could try twenty seconds of power walk followed by ten seconds of resting walk. Then build it up to longer power walks, followed by a rest. Over time, you will build your endurance and fitness levels, and you will become a walking queen, feeling young and free. I have found walking to be one of the most creative, meditative spaces. It's a wonderful way to process what is going on inside the body, mind, and spirit. It's great for stress relief. It's a wonderful way to get your daily dose of endorphins. What I have always loved about walking, which I started from a young age, was that no matter how bad I felt within, I could always go for a walk. It cost me nothing, and I could always feel good. I still love how walking makes me feel, and it doesn't matter whether you come from money; walking doesn't separate us. I truly believe if you can walk, it's an absolute gift, because for those who cannot walk, I am sure they would do anything in this world to have the opportunity. When I go for a walk, I am grateful that I have this blessed, natural ability to make myself feel good through walking.

Day 11 — Eat, Pray, Love

Today is inspired by the very beautiful and amazing author Elizabeth Gilbert, of *Eat, Pray, Love*. It's one of my favourite books, as well as inspirational authors.

Eat

Try your best today to eat healthy, unprocessed foods. Choose natural, healthy foods that nourish you.

Take the time to connect with yourself mindfully when you take your food. Before it has entered your mouth, think about if what you are about to eat is full of vitamins and minerals that will benefit your health. Or is the food you are about to eat going to take you away from being the best version of yourself? It wasn't until I started mindfully eating that I could overcome my emotional eating of processed foods.

When you take the time to pause, focus on your breath and sit back for a moment. Be the observer of the food you are about to eat. You can truly assess whether what you are about to eat will benefit your health and well-being. Will the food you are about to eat will take you further away from being the best, healthiest, and happiest version of your true self?

Take the time to eat mindfully. Chew your food. Choose fresh fruits and vegetables, and foods that are the colours of the rainbow. Take the time to eat. Instead of trying to eat at the same time you are working at your desk, become fully present. Sit down to eat your breakfast, lunch, snacks, or dinner; do that one thing. Eating at that time will also help with your body and mind to connect to the fact that right now, you are eating, and you are choosing to nourish yourself inside and out. The work will be there waiting for you after you eat.

When you eat, become present. That's the key: know what you are eating, and why. Connect with yourself when you eat. Become present in your body, mind, and spirit when you eat. Take the time to slow down, and don't rush what you are eating.

Pray

Ground yourself for a moment and become present within. You can sit anywhere, or roll out your yoga mat. Pray for the well-being of other people and yourself. Put a prayer out there to the universe for someone who might need the universe's help. Pray for others and for yourself. Say a prayer for something you truly want for either yourself or someone else.

I like to always bring my hands into pray position, close my eyes, and take a big breath in through my nose and out through my nose. That's when I centre myself and become fully present. That's also the time when I am grateful for being fully present and taking the time to pray and send out loving thoughts to others worldwide. I truly believe when you give love and care for others, the universe always has your back. If you haven't said a prayer in a very long time, or never, here is one of my little prayers I want to share with you that you can use.

I pray for others suffering. I hope they feel better soon and get all the love and support they can. I pray for my own health and wellness, so I can share my own love and light to help others.

You have the power to create any prayer you want. Pray to any higher gods, universe, or high powers you wish; there is no right or wrong. You simply have to pray for others and yourself, and send out beautiful, positive, kind, caring, compassionate thoughts, energy, and vibes to the universe. This is when your whole world will change and open. I truly believe when you go about each day caring about the love and well-being of others, what you get back from the universe far outweighs any money you could ever receive. Make it your own, and pray for whatever you want.

Love

Wake up in the morning and love yourself. Look in the mirror and take a moment to appreciate how beautiful you are, just the way you are. Say out loud, "I am love, I am love. I love myself." This might be one of the most challenging things to do throughout this wellness program, but self-love is key and this very simple and effective self-love practice that actually comes from Louise Hay will make you feel your own love from within.

When you connect with your inner self and come from a place of love, it will light up your world and change the way you feel inside. You will find peace within, and the struggle of self-hate will be over. You will feel healthy, happy, and free. When we feel loved, we can then also share that love with other people. Another thing you can do today for love is when you're driving and someone cuts you off. Instead of sending them angry, frustrated thoughts and energy, send them some love. You never know what is going on in others' world; perhaps people are nearly losing their family houses, or their jobs, so they are in such a hurry to get to work because it is desperate times. It's still no excuse for cutting you off, but you never know what is going on with people. Instead of jumping straight to the "I hate you" angry mode, send them some loving, healing thoughts. It will not only make you feel better and reduce the road rage, but when you put out love, you will receive it back ten times more.

Day 12 — Get Your Beauty Sleep

Deepak Chopra and Kimberly Synder talk about beauty sleep and about how important getting sleep is in their *Radical Beauty Book*. From my own experience, I know all too well how amazing I feel after I get eight hours of sleep—and I know how terrible I feel if I don't enough sleep.

Getting eight hours of sleep a night will make the biggest difference to your own health and well-being. When you wake up after getting eight hours of sleep, you wake up feeling great and ready to take on the day. However, if you don't get a good night's sleep, you wake up wanting to do nothing but lie in bed.

Aim each night to get eight hours' sleep. Make this a non-negotiable because it is when we are asleep that our brains are repairing, and our whole system has the much-needed rest and repair it needs in order for us to function as human beings.

If you want to become your happiest, healthiest, spiritual self, you need to do your best and aim to get eight hours of sleep a night. It's really as simple as that.

As a blogger, I can fall into bad habits, and there have been times that I have stayed up past my bedtime. Because I had been working at a day job and then working my blog on the side, I would find myself blogging before or after work. Then I fell into a bad habit of blogging at night, trying to cram in everything I needed to do in order to build my blog so it could go from being just another blogger to a professional blogger. I must admit that staying up late, trying to cram in everything at night, and working long hours didn't serve my highest good. Before too long, it started to affect my health and wellness, and the way I felt. Over time, I think it contributed me to getting writer's block and not being as creatively energized as I used to be.

I now do my very best to get eight hours' worth of sleep. An hour before I go to bed, I dim the lights and make sure I am not looking at my mobile phone and social media. That took a lot of practice because as a global spa and wellness blogger, I have people constantly commenting or sending me messages or e-mails, and I used to feel obligated to get back to each and every person. Now I realize how important my sleep is. Without my sleep, I can't possibly be the best version of myself, and if I can't make the time to sleep and put my health first, then Spa It Girl and living the life of my dreams wouldn't be possible. Sleep is so important if you want to become your happiest, healthiest, spiritual self. Even though it can be tempting to work on your dreams past your bedtime, I recommended working on your health and wellness first, and getting eight hours sleep. You will then wake up the next day feeling so great and able to set your intentions, meditate, be active, and choose healthy and nourishing things. You will feel like you have so much energy and feel so much better, and it will take you less time to do the things you need to do because you are not exhausted.

I now realize that it doesn't matter how late I stay up each night; the to-do list will always be there. I make sure that at the top of my to-do list each night is to get eight hours of beauty sleep. When I get a good night's sleep, I always wake up feeling great, inspired, and excited to be active and eat healthy. I feel happy, and I deal with the pressures of the day better. I feel so much more positive because I have the energy I need. My body, mind, and spirit have to rest and repair at night. This truly does make a difference.

It is one of my go-to wellness tips: make sure you get your eight hours of beauty sleep!

One thing I learnt while going on a wellness retreat to Gwinganna (which I recommend) was how drinking coffee after noon can hinder my natural ability to fall asleep at night. When I applied this basic principle of having a cup of coffee only in the morning, and after that switching to black tea, it made an immense difference in getting to sleep at night. I felt my thoughts were not overactive, and I felt much more relaxed. I was still doing the same exercise and eating healthy. The only difference I made to my day was cutting out drinking coffee after noon, and it worked.

If you are finding it hard to get your eight hours of beauty sleep, drinking your coffee only in the morning, and then from noon onwards, switch to drinking caffeine-free herbal tea, or any tea that will also give you that little pick-me-up caffeine you need, but without the heart-thumping junkie buzz that coffee gives you. At my recent wellness retreat at COMO Shambhala Estate in Bali, I had the pleasure of meeting with their wellness consultant, Nancy, who also recommended switching to tea in the afternoon. I am always searching energy when working long hours. I've also found when I drink too much coffee, it's not great for my digestive system. My doctor said that anyone struggling with irritable bowel syndrome should cut out drinking coffee totally, because it can upset the digestive system. Each of us is different, so if you are having a lot of trouble and are not able to sleep, I suggest visiting your doctor first to discuss your concerns. In the meantime, you can try healthy lifestyle tips to see if any help you like they helped me.

So how do you get a good night's sleep? Here are my go-to beauty sleep tips to help you.

Invest in a good bed that is perfect for what you need. If you are sleeping in a crappy, old bed that is sagging in the middle, and you are waking up with a sore back or feeling like you haven't been to sleep, it's time for you to think about investing in a good bed. That way you can get some proper sleep and not wake up feeling sore and in pain.

For many years, I slept in beds at the lower end of quality—the cheapest mattress I could find. It was great on my pocketbook, but it wasn't great for my back or hips, and I would wake up feeling like I hadn't been to bed.

When I used to climb into bed, I went through stages of thinking, "I need a new bed. This bed is so uncomfortable." When your inner self is telling you this, it's time for a new bed that will serve your highest good.

When I finally got the bed that I like to call my dream, every time I climb into my bed, it makes me feel good, and I want to drift away to my resting place. It's nice and comfy, but it also gives me the support I need. Ever since investing in a proper mattress, the most important thing I needed (sleep) has finally been achieved. I recommend checking in with how you are feeling when going to bed, while in bed, and when waking up. Then make any changes accordingly.

If it's time for you to get a new bed, focus on how much you might need to save, and go for it. Getting good quality, deep sleep is essential to your health.

Next, make sure your bedroom is clean and clutter free, so you can walk around freely. Make sure it's dust-free, and that you have either clean carpet or floors. Give it a little overhaul because you want to create the luxurious, dreamy sleep environment. Have soft colours on your bed, as well as soft, inviting sheets to make you feel good and are nice to touch. Have the right pillows. There is no point in having a pillow on your bed that is uncomfortable. Invest the time to focus on what pillow you will put under your head.

When your room is clean, soft, and pretty, then from the moment you walk in the door and it's time to have a shower and go to bed, your bedroom is inviting you into a sweet dreams state.

I find I can't get a good night's sleep if my room is messy and cluttered, or if the cover and sheets are not soft and inviting. Also, get the room temperature right. If you are lucky enough to open a window to get fresh air, that's even better.

I like a nice, warm shower before I go to bed. I like to do my skincare, brush my teeth, and settle into some inspiring, feel-good pyjamas. I make sure that when I am in my en-suite that connects to my room, my lights are off in my bedroom, and can I switch into my sleep mode.

Another thing I have found that is beneficial to getting a good night's sleep is switching off the TV two hours before I go to bed. I take time out to lie down on my couch and relax with low lights. This atmosphere makes me sleepy naturally.

If I stay up too late on my computer, it wires me, and I can't switch off and go to sleep. I recommend limiting your computer usage and mobile phone usage at night. When you talk to people online through messenger, before you know it, you have been up for hours, and you are wide awake and can't get to sleep. As a rule of thumb, I try my best to have 8:30 p.m. as my cut-off point for being connected with all my techno devices. It doesn't work every time, depending on different work deadlines. However, as a basis, create your own go-to-sleep routine. Add beautiful lighting and relaxation music. Try yoga for sleep, or a guided mediation for sleep. Create your own It Girl beauty sleep routine and stick with it!

Work out when you need to wake up the next morning, and then count back eight hours from there; that will give you what time you need to be in bed. Once you established a regular routine of when you need to get up and when you need to go to bed, your body will get used to it over time.

I truly believe when you can get eight hours of sleep, the beauty sleep does wonders on how you feel. It allows you to have the energy to wake up and exercise to be a go-getter.

It also helps you better deal with stress throughout the day because you are not tired, cranky, and struggling through the day.

Getting enough sleep can help improve your eating habits and reduce your stress levels. It can reduce dark under-eye circles and give you clearer skin. I truly believe it's key if you want to become your best, healthy, happy self.

Day 13 — Everywhere You Go, Always Take Water with You

Drink lots of water. Everywhere you go, take water with you. Drink it out of a BPA or glass bottle, and carry it around with you in your handbag. I never leave home without carrying water, and I encourage you to do the same thing. When you are at home, I recommend drinking water out of a glass. This will help with reducing those fine lines and wrinkles you get from sucking water out of a bottle. When you work out, drink lots of water before so that you are well hydrated throughout, and especially afterwards. Drink more water than cups of coffee and tea. If you are feeling tired, instead of reaching for a fizzy soft drink, reach for another glass of water. If you find you are constantly hungry, it might not be that you are hungry, but you are simply thirsty.

My go-to wellness Spa It Girl tip is to drink lots of water. We are about 70 per cent water, and so without water, we cannot function at our best. When you drink lots of water, it makes you feel good. You don't feel as hungry all the time, and you feel well-hydrated. It does wonders for your health and skin. If you don't like the taste of water, then try adding some fresh lemon or lime to it, or even fresh fruit like strawberries and oranges. Get creative and find a way to fall in love with drinking water daily.

Day 14 — Make Every Day Like Self-love Sunday

Love yourself unconditionally. Tell yourself how much you love yourself, and express what you love most about yourself. If you find yourself having negative, self-hate thoughts, send yourself some kind, self-love thoughts and positive energy instead.

You are a loving, beautiful soul. You have all the love you need, and it comes from within. Today, choose to do things that make you feel loved and nurtured from within. Love yourself no matter what; accept yourself for who you are, as you are.

Don't wait till you become that perfect dress size or body shape—love yourself today. If you are not used to focusing on yourself and doing things for yourself because you are normally focussing your attention on everyone else here are a few ideas to get you started.

- Take a nice, long shower or warm, relaxing bath.
- Lie by the beach and then go for a swim.
- Read a feel-good book.
- Have a massage.
- Book a spa treatment and visit a day spa.

- Practice restorative yoga; take time to hold the stretch and breathe through any tension.
- Do a guided meditation for relaxation.
- Lie on the couch and get off your mobile phone; simply be, relax, unwind, and watch a feel-good movie.
- Buy yourself a bunch of flowers.
- Write yourself a self-love letter.
- Get a haircut, so you can get a relaxing shampoo and conditioner head massage.
- Light a candle and take time to smell the scent.
- Listen to relaxation music.
- Exercise to feel good.
- Eat healthy, nourishing food.
- Pop on a facemask.

There are so many things to choose from, and as long as you love yourself and it makes you feel good, that's all that matters. Take the time today to rest, relax, and nurture yourself. Treasure how beautiful you are. Be grateful for this very special self-love day and every kind, loving, peaceful, relaxing moment.

When you take the time to read the morning paper, eat your breakfast, or have your cup of tea, be grateful that every Sunday is your self-love Sunday. It's a day you focus your attention inwards and to love yourself whole heartily and unconditionally.

Take a self-love Sunday selfie, add #iamaspaitgirl, and tag @spaitgirl. Write about what self-love Sunday means to you and why others should join you too.

Self-love starts from within, and the only person who can make self-love happen within is you.

Day 15 — Meditation Monday

I remember growing up as a kid and listening to the Bangles song "Manic Monday." At the time I didn't quite know what that really meant, but now that I am much older, I know what they meant.

When you have just had the pleasure of a couple of days off to yourself, and you have been able to do your own thing, you are only human if, on Monday, you wish it was Sunday.

Sometimes on a Sunday night, you can find yourself having this inner dialogue: "I don't want to go to work tomorrow. Why does the weekend have to go so quickly? Why do I have to work? Oh, no, I have to go back to work tomorrow." It can play over and over, and if you are not working in your dream job and it's the complete opposite, the thought of even thinking about doing back to work on a Monday can bring all sorts of negative emotions. Then when you wake up on a Monday morning, and it can make you feel even worse. You may even experience the Monday blues. It's quite common for people who are working in a job they are not passionate about, just doing it for the money. I know because I have been there and have dreaded the Monday morning alarm.

If I had my spiritual girl power way, I would go to the man-made money machine and print out pages and pages of paper notes. Then I'd throw it out in the streets so everyone could be free of having to work just for money and to make a living. But of course, that is wishful thinking.

What do you do if you aren't working in your dream job right now, or you aren't living the life of your dreams because you are busy trying to create it and manifest it? You change the way you feel by meditating, and you focus on having a meditation Monday instead.

First you need to create space within. Find a quiet, comfortable place; it can be in bed or when you get out of bed. Focus your attention inwards, close your eyes, and listen to your breath, practice taking nice deep long breaths in through the nose and then out through the mouth.

There is no right way or wrong way when it comes to meditating; do whatever feels natural and go with the flow of your own breath. Start your day by connecting with your true inner self and like always setting your daily intention.

Some people love Mondays because they might have the day off or because they are waking up to live their passion and dreams.

Other people might hate Mondays because they don't have the day off and feel like the weekend went too quickly. They feel they didn't have enough time for themselves.

If I had my way, every workplace would be a four-days-per-week operation. I know how busy life can be, and it's only human to feel like your life is out of balance because you only get two days to relax and for yourself, and then you have to come back and do it all again, working five full days.

Even though it's a Monday and you might have to go back to work, it's important to practice self-love. Your happiness, health, and wellness still have to come first.

Taking care of yourself is so important, especially when you are personally suffering from the Monday blues. Your health is so important, and doing things to make yourself feel good is key.

If you are finding that you get too distracted meditating on your own, then try a guided meditation through YouTube or an app. Whenever you feel the Monday blues, or you wake up wishing you could stay in bed all day, meditate and create space within.

Day 16 — Smile, Smile, Smile

You will probably notice, by looking at my Instagram page (@Spaitgirl) or Facebook page (Spa It Girl), that I love to smile. The reason I love to smile is because it makes me feel good. I discovered from a very young age it makes others feel good too. I find smiling to be a beautiful, kind-hearted greeting, and it sometimes speaks louder than words.

I started smiling from a young age, and I think that's because it always made me feel happy. Plus, I felt like it was a gesture of kindness and was a way of being kind without saying a word.

If you want to change the way you feel, then my number one go-to tip is to smile, smile, smile. It will change the way you feel and will lift your mood. When you smile it will make you feel good, and others too.

I remember travelling on the London Underground Tube and noticing that people didn't smile at each other, even though they were so close to other. The other thing I noticed was that no one attempted to even make eye contact. No sooner was someone about to get off the seat than another person was right behind, angling to take that seat.

When I first arrived to London and started catching the Underground, I felt like this little, bouncing, young, happy Aussie kangaroo, eager to smile, say hello, and be kind. Before long I realised that wasn't a very cool thing to do on the way to work on the London Underground. In order to fit in so people wouldn't think I was crazy, I did not smile or be kind. It was a dog eat dog world every day, and it was not cool to smile, smirk, or be outgoing and kind.

If I had any words of wisdom for my younger self, it would be: When you live in one of the world's greyest places, you need to smile, smile, smile and be kind. When you smile, it makes you feel good, as well as everyone else around you.

If I had one wish for everyone who travels on any major city public transport, it is when someone looks at you, say hello with your beautiful, feel-good smile. Doing that can change the way you feel.

Despite what country I am travelling in and how packed out the public transport is, I smile. I choose to smile because I want to make myself feel good. I've been there and done that, after living in London and changing the way I felt. I made myself even feel more depressed. I wouldn't recommend it to anyone.

I have met so many amazing people simply through smiling. Some of my best friends have come from my smiling at them and then having a conversation. I met actually one of my walking besties simply by smiling one day. We got to talking about walking from that simple smile and conversation. Years later, we are still in contact all the time, and we still go walking up a hill, which was one of the first conversations we had. We realised that we had been walking up the same hill, and we should do it together sometime. There have been so many times when I have met people in coffee shops, airports, or working out—all from a simple smile.

If you want to become more spiritual, smile more. It's like giving someone a feel-good hug. Also, being spiritual isn't just about practicing yoga and meditation; it is about the experiences and also the people you meet. You can become so rich spiritually by travelling the world and by smiling at stranger. You might get to meet, and before you know it, you have just been told the most amazing places to visit, shop, or see. I get so many amazing insider tips as a global spa and wellness blogger, and it's all from smiling. I also get to meet the most amazing people who are now part of my life.

I have tried to fit into some places like London, and I didn't express my beautiful, kind, loving, smiling self. It left me feeling down, and I didn't get to meet anyone while I was on the London Underground because talking and smiling was discouraged.

I can't help thinking how beautiful the world would be with everyone smiling in person and in photos. How kind, loving, and compassionate the world would be with others smiling as a gesture of kindness. I invite you today to smile, smile, smile—both at yourself and at others.

Smiling will always make you feel good no matter what, and it will bring you back to your true, authentic self. Think back to when you were a kid. Did you love smiling then? If you did start smiling, don't let societies and stereotyping influence you now that you are an adult. I encourage all people to change their mindsets to "Yes, I am an adult, but I choose to smile because it makes me feel good." The more smiling you can do, the better you will feel inside and out.

You want to always smile on the inside, so keep checking with yourself. Are you smiling on the inside? Or have lost your smile? If you don't feel happy inside and are not your usual, happy self inside and out, make sure that when something doesn't feel quite right inside, you have a medical check-up and talk to someone. You always want to feel happy inside. It's not going to be every minute of the day, because we are all human, but you do want to feel your inner smile, knowing that you have a real interest in your own life.

I invite you to look at your beautiful smile in the mirror and shine. I also invite you to smile, smile, smile at yourself and at others. Even if things go pear-shaped or off the rails, that's okay because you always have your smile to come back to, and that will make you feel great no matter what.

When you are taking public transportation, smile. Chances are when someone looks back at you, he or she might smile too. If people don't, that's okay. Then you might break out into laughter, because it's so funny when you are the only one choosing to express your birthright of happiness, love, light, and kindness.

When you smile, it will make you feel good from within. Regardless of the environment you are, in never suppress your happiness or the way you feel. Always express yourself, because suppressing the way you truly feel can lead to making you feel down and not your happiest self.

Day 17 — Workout Wednesday

Wednesday has to be my go-to-favourite day of the working week. It's known as hump day, and I think subconsciously we all know that we are halfway through the week, so we start to feel good.

I love to work out every single Wednesday—hail, rain, or sunshine. If for some reason you get caught up on Monday or Tuesday and didn't exercise, it's best not to beat yourself up. Make every Wednesday a workout Wednesday.

When it comes to working out, I believe it's important to find a way to move that makes you feel good. I love to move by practicing yoga, walking, or doing a Les Mills body attack class. Everyone has her own way she likes to move.

I recommend trying lots of different activities, workout classes, outdoor or indoor sports, different yoga styles, and different yoga teachers. Eventually you will find a way to move that makes you feel good.

When you work out, even though it's hard work, you are going to feel good and raise your endorphins. It's about taking care of your health and happiness. I truly believe in this day and age, it's the key to our happiest self, and even survival. Exercising has so many health benefits for the body, mind, and spirit. It's a great way to prevent serious diseases and illnesses. Making time to work out and feel good is win-win.

If you find it hard to get motivated, find a support network to help you. I have been lucky to have a close bestie who always contacts me, asking me to meet her to go for a walk. Sometimes it's even on my days off, and all I can think is, *Oh, goodness. It's so early, and she wants to catch up!*

But after I meet up with her and go for a walk, and we chat, laugh, and have a ball, I am high on natural, feel-good endorphins. I feel amazing within. I always tell her, "Thanks for inviting me and pushing me. There is no way I would have got out of bed this morning, on my day off, to do this epic walk up a hill had you not asked me."

One of my besties even gets me up early on New Year's Day, to walk a hill. My younger party girl self in her twenties would say, "There is no way I am walking up a hill on New Year's Day!" But my new, sensible, spiritual girl in her late thirties says, "Okay, wow. Let's do this! I want to wake up on New Year's Day and feel great!" This is now our New Year's ritual: waking up, feeling great, being alcohol free, and being active it girls who walk up a hill. Every New Year's Day for me, no matter where I am, that is my ritual. I truly believe it sets my intention for the rest of the year, and I love the way it makes me feel.

If ever get invited to work out with someone else, I take them up on the offer. Sometimes all you need is your workout buddy to support you in moving. Even though I am a qualified personal trainer and fitness instructor, I am going to be completely honest: I have some days when my thoughts are telling me I can't be bothered to exercise today as it's been such a long day at work. However, then I think to myself, "There is a body attack class on at the gym after work. If I go, I will be able to socialise and see others, listen to fantastic music, and be motivated to move by my amazing Les Mills teacher." I find that it's the best way to de-stress after a long day, and I always feel great after the class is done. When I am doing the class, focussing on the moves, getting into the groove, and not running into anyone, then I tend to loosen up, smile, laugh, sing and have fun. It's the best feeling ever.

In the past, I tried workouts that I didn't like for whatever reason. They didn't click with me, or they didn't make me feel passionately in love with it. Had I not kept searching for what makes me feel good inside, discovering a workout that I couldn't do without, I would still be a my unhealthy self. Find a workout you love and that makes you feel good within. Once you fall in love with what makes you happy, when it comes to your own moves, you will never want to give up that feel-good feeling. I truly believe that's the secret to maintaining an active life: finding what makes you want to move, and what moves you. I have also even started to try exercise more in the morning, and I have found if I exercise before I start work, then it's definitely done. If I am feeling tired after a big day at work, I don't have to make excuses. When you start your day with exercise in the morning, it also helps set your day, and you get the best dose of feel-good endorphins and energy. Finding a time and place to exercise that suits your lifestyle is key.

I invite you to move in a way that makes you feel good. Enjoy your workout Wednesday. If you are stuck inside all day because it's cold and raining, or if you don't have anyone to mind the kids, that's okay. Simply walk in place, and then do some walking lunges around your house. Try a YouTube workout. Involve your kids if you need to! Invest in a hula hoop, a yoga mat, a skipping rope, and a couple of light hand weights. Create your own workout moves because you have the power within to move, move, move and change the way you feel.

Day 18 — Tap into Your Inner Kid

A lot of people tell me I don't look my age. They almost fall over when I tell them I am nearly forty. I think it's funny at times because some people think I am in my late twenties or early thirties. I have to tell them I'm almost forty, and from there they are fascinated and want to know some of the things I do so they too can look and feel youthful.

When you spend a little bit of time each day tapping into your inner kid, it helps with changing the way you feel and lightening the heavy, doom-and-gloom world in which we live.

When we become adults, it's like society tells us we must act a certain way. If we're acting like kids and having fun, there can be a social stigma still to this day that we have gone crazy. But the only thing that is crazy is that someone's own thought has influenced generations and society in us having fun as Adults and acting kid like which makes you feel good inside. I now make sure that I don't suppress the way I feel. I used to try to act sensibly, grown-up, and stiff, like society expects adults should be. But I soon found out living like this and suppressing my happiness made me unhappy.

I believe it's important to tap into your inner kid to do things that light you up and make you feel good inside. If you used to sing into a hairbrush to your favourite song, then do it now. If you used to love doing cartwheels in a park, find a park and do them. If you used to love to walk or run, do it. If you have had a lifelong dream—in my case, to travel the world and to write a book—do it! Tapping into your inner kid is about tapping into your true, authentic self. When you start to live within your true, authentic spirit and express yourself, it's the best feeling ever because you no longer wonder, "Who am I? What do I need to do to make myself happy?" If you want to change the way you feel, tap into your inner child and start doing all the things you loved doing as a kid. It will make you feel young and youthful, and it does wonders for your skin, health, and happiness. Don't go out of your way to make yourself unhappy; instead, cast aside what society tells you about how you should act.

You only have to look at Ellen DeGeneres to gain some true inspiration. Dancing and being happy can make you feel happy and youthful, as well as everyone else around you.

In Australia we have these two amazing comedians, Hamish and Andy who are on the radio and when I am driving home from work in my car they always make me laugh out loud, they both really know how to tap into their inner kid and how to have fun.

When I am with my two nieces I am open to tapping into my inner kid and have so much fun with them and I can do anything from singing out loud, dancing, hula hooping, art work, being creative, social and yes even joining into their musically routines which they think is totally hilarious.

I have so much fun with them and they always make me laugh out loud, smile and feel good within, I truly do love them both to bits.

In society we might be expected to act a certain way when we become a certain age, however if we choose to follow some of these right old age social stigmas it can suppress our own happiness and even make us feel depressed.

I think it's important to tap into your inner kid and when you feel happy choose to connect with it and express it rather then worry about what other people will think of you and it's also important to remember you are not crazy should you choose to sing out loud in your car or in a department store to your favourite song you are simply being a human being.

Let's face it no one thinks Beyonce' or Katy Perry is crazy for singing out loud in public so why should it be any different for ourselves and others. Be the change and connect with your own happiness that comes from within and as it arises let it vibrate and shine.

Today, I invite you to write a list of things you loved to do as a kid. From that list, tick the things you are already doing.

With the things that are not ticked on your list, start doing them! Always make time to tap into your inner kid, and get ready to feel how amazing it is. There is a whole lot of love, happiness, and joy waiting inside you, ready to bubble out and flow over you.

Day 19 — Become Bigger Than Your Fears, and Forgive

I have found that holding on to my fears (or someone else's influenced fear, because I was a kid and was too little to understand and process things) can hold me back from living my dreams and having amazing life experiences. Holding onto fear also can bring with it negative energy, anxieties, and emotions that don't make us feel all that good; rather, they make us unsettled and sometimes even panic us.

If you want to work on becoming your healthiest and happiest self, one of the key things is to figure out whether you are holding on to any fears. The next challenge is to become bigger than your fears, because when you become bigger than your fears and live your fears, it is the most liberating feeling.

You might have a fear that lives deep inside you. Everyone has different fears, and what is a fear to someone might be considered a joy to someone else. For example, when someone says flying, you might instantly fear it; the thought of it makes you sick. However, someone else might love it so much that she can't wait to plan her next holiday and fly to some other part of the world.

To become bigger than our fears, first we must get to the core of what our fears are. I invite you to pick up a piece of paper and write down every single fear you have. Beside that list, write down where you think each fear came from. Did it come from someone you knew while growing up? From the TV? From a kid at school? Were you involved in some sort of scare? Spend some time diving into this fear. Sometimes even writing about your fears and thinking about them can be enough to bring on fearful emotions. Go with ease and breathe.

- What do I fear?
- Why do I fear it?

This might come as quite a surprise considering I love to travel around the world and visit luxury day spa hotels, resorts, and retreats. I even used to live in London, and from there I travelled the world nearly every weekend. However, in my case, I feared flying to Bali.

Why? Because as a small kid (and even as a teenager), I grew up in a small country town. Some older ladies had heard on the media how corrupt Bali was, and how it wasn't safe to travel there as a woman. Even though lots of Aussie families were travelling there and bringing back cheap videos and imitation designer clothes, a majority of the older ladies in my town swore that Bali wasn't safe. Of course, we would see horrible footage on TV of everything that could go wrong, and it would strengthen the fear.

Bali also had this stereotype back in the eighties where it was just for young, drunken louts. I didn't feel like I fitted into the category, and that also strengthened my fear. There were Aussies shown on the news not behaving themselves in Bali and the consequences that went with that. It seemed to be like this ongoing negative cycle of thoughts and feelings. When another major incident happened in Bali, it was another way my fear was strengthened.

You could apply this to any fear that you have, and perhaps you can also reflect back to developing a fear from a young age that was actually a fear of someone else's, but because you were little and unable to make up your own mind, you believed in that fear. Also, perhaps you looked up to the person as a role model. In my case, they hadn't even travelled to Bali. As an adult, you have to question your fears. Seriously, how would those ladies know? It was easy to latch on to a negative story that might come out of one country, and to never hear all of the beautiful things that were happening.

The news likes to showcase all of the horrible things. News shows were created to make you feel good, yet they showcase all of the things that are wrong with the world, all of the tragic events that go on. If you want to make yourself feel down, then all you need to do is turn on the news. If you want to make yourself feel good, turn on your favourite music. I now have seen my own nieces hear something on the news and develop a fear. I try to talk to them one-on-one to help them understand that it doesn't happen everywhere.

If I have learnt one thing over my own personal spiritual journey, it's that quite often your fears are someone else's. When we have kids around us, we should never express our own fears. We should own our fears and become bigger than them, because all we do by expressing our fears in front of little kids is pass the fears on. Then a little kid turns into an adult but can still be carrying that fear years later.

If you feel like you have been holding onto a fear from a very young age, then I invite you to become bigger than your fear. Choose just one fear to work on. Then write down all the practical reasons why, as an adult with all your facts and knowledge, you know why your fear is not true. Acknowledge that the fear is no longer your fear to hold onto; it was never your fear in the first place. Now put together an action plan for overcoming your fear.

An example is if your fear is flying, because someone else saw something on TV and then told you all the bad things about flying. That now means you haven't been able to fly anywhere, because you have always associated the thought of flying with negative feelings, emotions, and outright panic. Now is the time to write down, "I choose to become bigger than my fear. Flying can no longer hurt me."

Work out a time and place to go on a flight. Make it a small one to start with, because even though say you are ready to do it, you might freeze up when you get on the plane. Practicing your meditation daily and learning how to breathe your way through anxiety will help. Add a mantra: "Everything is going to be all right. I am safe. It's okay to fly."

You can apply these same principles to any of your fears. Over time, you will let go of the fears that you have been holding. They have been holding you back from living your best, happiest, healthiest, spiritual life.

Before too long, you will love flying so much that you will wonder why you ever feared it. The more you become bigger with the fears, the more confident you will be. Without realizing it, when you have a fear that lives deep inside you, it's a burden that you have to live with, and sometimes you can't even make sense of why are you so fearful about it. This is because there is a risk or a chance you can get hurt, and you don't want to be hurt.

Working on your own fears and becoming bigger than them isn't an exercise that you will overcome in one day. It is going to take a bit of practice. By taking the time to first acknowledge what your fears are and why, and which fear you want to become bigger than, you'll have taken the first step in transforming your life. Becoming bigger than you fears will make you feel uncomfortable at times. It's important to remember to always breathe through it and repeat the mantra: "I am safe, and everything is going to be okay."

Now that you know a little bit more about why it's good to work on becoming bigger than your fears, if you want to work even further on the first fear, here are some more questions to answer. They will help you get to the core of becoming bigger than your fears.

- Where did this fear come from? Who influenced it?
- How long have you held on to this fear?
- How do you know the fear is true, if you have never personally done it before?
- How many times does this fear happen to other people in a day, week, month, lifetime?
- Now that you are older and wiser, do you believe this fear is real? Or are you still holding onto other people's thoughts, beliefs, and fears?
- What can you do to overcome your fear?

In my experience, if you have a fear, the only way to overcome it is to not believe in it and to live your fear. Fear doesn't serve your highest good; it simply makes you feel unsafe, unsettled, scared, and fearful inside. These are all negative emotions that are only going for holding you back feeling good and living your dreams.

All you need to do is believe you can become bigger than your fears. There is so much to look forward to when you overcome your fears, so be patient and work on it. With self-belief, you can overcome anything! By overcoming your fears, you can unlock a new way of life and a world that you have been missing out on, all because you had been living in fear.

Forgiveness

Let's face it: we all can relate to having someone in our lives who we feel has either done us wrong, didn't treat us the way we deserved to be treated, or made us feel horrible. We simply don't want to forgive the person. But as easy as it is to hold a grudge, it doesn't get you anywhere. It simply makes you feel sick or angry every time you hear that person's name.

So what's my number one tip? Forgive everyone, even that person you never thought you could forgive.

It took me years to work this out. I was making myself feel upset and angry because I was holding on to past hurts of how others had treated me. The only person I was hurting in this process of holding on to a grudge or disliking someone was me.

If you want to change the way you feel, then the first thing you must do is make peace with the hurt, and with the past that you are emotionally holding within your body, mind, and spirit.

So how do you forgive? Well, it's not something that I just put out there in one sentence: "I forgive …" and then *poof!* the anger and hurt were gone. Instead, I had to work at it.

I started doing some yoga practices for a broken heart. In my case, it had to do with past relationships that didn't work out. At the time, I felt that I deserved better. I started focusing inwards and doing yoga lotus poses to open up my hips and start working on the emotional pain within. I tend to hold in a lot of emotional pain. Then when someone mentioned that person's name, or I had to bump into him unexpectedly, I repeated the mantra, "I forgive, I forgive." I also made peace with a quote that I heard from Oprah Winfrey: "I didn't know then what I know now."

I actually forgave myself, in order to forgive someone else. I had to forgive myself first because at the time, I was my younger self and was trying to make sense of the world; I couldn't make of who I was back then. I was lost and confused, and perhaps as a result, I didn't always pick the best people with whom to be in a relationship. But once I forgave myself for not knowing what was best, I thanked the universe for showing me the way, and I forgave the other person. I felt it was time to let go of the past and fully surrender to it. I never had to have that horrible experience and reminder of that person in my life; I was able to let go, and I freed myself from the past hurt and pain. I then gave up all the emotional thoughts, feelings, and energies within myself. It truly did change the way I felt.

I now know holding on to anything that doesn't serve your highest good is not worth holding on to at all. It only holds you back from living your healthiest, happiest life. So ask yourself, "Who do I need to forgive?" Think about why you need to forgive yourself. Was it because you didn't know then what you know now?

Forgive yourself for making any choices you now know you wouldn't make, because you know better. We are all going to go into things with our best intentions—marriages, relationships, new jobs, new businesses. In an ideal world within our head, we would love to plan and control things so that everything goes to our plan. It doesn't mean that it will always go well, though. Remember that the universe is guiding you, and every step back is a redirection. If it were meant to be, it would have been. I have a saying every time things go pear-shaped in my life. My mantra is, "The universe has bigger plans for me!"

Repeat this mantra every time things go pear-shaped in your own life. Remember to forgive and let go of any past hurts.

This will change the way you feel, and by forgiving others and yourself, it will bring you closer to your true, authentic loving self. You'll start feeling love instead of hatred towards yourself and others. That is the key to living a healthy, happy, spiritual life.

Day 20 — Connect to Your Inner Self and Your True, Authentic Passion That Comes from Within

I believe each and every one of us has a passion, a purpose, a talent (or many talents), and a gift. It's simply about tuning in and following what already comes from within.

In order to live your passion, you need to know what your passion is, and you need to make it clear. If you spend some time each day cultivating your spiritual practice through your yoga practice, mindfulness, and mediation, asking questions to the universe and your higher self when you are on the yoga mat, all the questions will come from within. Don't stress out if you don't get the answer when you first ask the questions. Come back each day and strengthen your spiritual practice, and all the answers to your questions will come from within. Everything you need comes from within. Unlocking and living your life to your full potential comes from within.

I tried for many years to live other people's dreams, or to live the socially accepted career. At the time, I was working in a corporate office, and the in thing to do was to climb the corporate ladder. I went from being a trainee to a full-time job at the reception desk, to the CEO's personal assistant. I then worked as secretariat assistant, project officer, project coordinator, and senior project coordinator for a top-notch, international, blue-chip company. I kept climbing the corporate ladder till I realised it didn't matter how far I climbed—this ladder didn't make me happy.

At the time, I was also working part-time in the fitness industry, teaching aerobics classes at many different gyms. Then I went on to become a personal trainer, but I always felt that I needed to keep my stable job because that was the sensible thing to do. To be honest, because I wasn't spending time with my yoga mat rolled out and connecting with my true inner self, I was confused as to what I wanted to do. I knew at the time I wanted to write a book, but I wasn't sure on what. I knew I loved going to the day spa and being active, but I didn't know how to pull it all together. If I had any words of wisdom for my younger self, it would be to roll out your yoga mat, be quiet, sit in silence, connect to your breath and your inner self, and listen. All the answers to my life purpose would come from within.

What's my life purpose? To feel good within, and to help others feel good too. It took me a long time to get this. However, I swear by creating space from within and making the time to cultivate your daily spiritual practice. All the answers to even the most confusing situations can be resolved internally, from simply asking the question and offering it up to the universe and your higher self. It's amazing how much can be resolved when you make the time to focus on your breath and become silent.

This is the sort of thing I wish they would have taught me in school. When you focus your attention inwards, all the answers you need will come from within, if you are quiet and listen.

I truly believe that if you want to live your healthiest, happiest, spiritual life, you have to do what makes you happy and what feels good within.

When I write, it doesn't feel like work. I am present, passionate, in the moment, and engaged—and I love it. I could write for hours or days, and it wouldn't feel like it. However, when I had to process account after account and do administration work, that felt like *real* work. We sat in one place, doing the same repetitive thing over and over in a small space, all sitting behind our computers and not talking to each other. We were there to work and were not being paid to socialise. That didn't resonate for me, and no matter how much I tried to make it work, deep inside, I knew I was not destined to be an office girl even though I had spent the last fifteen years or so trying to convince myself it was what I had to do. I ticked all the socially accepted boxes, but deep inside I wasn't happy. Going into the office became a drag, a chore, and a bore. It wasn't my passion, it wasn't my dream, and it didn't resonate with me.

Doing a job I didn't like affected the way I felt. It wasn't until I started living my true passion and dream, which made me feel good and in love with what I did, that I changed the way I felt.

There is nothing worse than waking up each day and hating what you have to do. It's not a good thing for your life to feel like a daily grind, or like you are stuck in a rut. I know all too well because I have been there and done that.

If you want to change the way you feel, make the time to ask yourself these simple questions.

- What do I want to do?
- What is it I truly love?
- What I am I passionate about?
- What makes me happy?

Then do whatever it takes to find a way to live your passion and your dreams. In my case, I wanted to write about luxury day spas, and though I couldn't get any paid writing gigs and I got so many knock-backs, I didn't let that stop me. Instead, I made a free Google Blogspot and started writing about day spas. Every day I woke up in the morning and creatively thought of which spa I would like to write about and feature. Before too long, without even realizing it, I was developing my own skills and gaining experience even if it was unpaid. I was living within my true, authentic self, within my passion, and I was following my dream.

I later went on to review luxury day spas, going from a free Google Blogspot to a dot-com, and I created an online global community of Spa It Girls from around the world.

There are now even boys who loved to visit day spas as much as I do.

I've now gone on to be recognised as one of the top luxury spa reviewers, writers, and wellness bloggers, being awarded and named as one of Australia's Top Fifty Influencers.

I truly believe none of this would be possible if I wasn't living my happy, healthy spiritual way of life. It wouldn't have happened if I had a job that didn't resonate with my inner soul.

I believe if you follow your own passion and dream, and if it comes from within, this is when the real magic happens. I have seen over the many years other people trying to live someone else's dream, and when they have tried to be like someone else or copied someone else's great idea or authentic style, it has never worked out. You can't live anyone else's dream other than your own—it's that simple.

If you want to live your dreams, you have to own it, and it has to come from within. It has to be your own passion, light up your heart and soul, and make you feel good within. Waking up daily to live your passion has to excite you and make you want to get out of bed. You also have to be prepared to work when you need to, and if you don't love what you do, then it's not going to serve your highest good.

When you are working towards living your dreams, there are going to be plenty of days, and even years when you won't get paid a cent and unless you are truly passionate about what you're doing and are clear on why you are doing it. I have seen people quit because the universe has a way of redirecting them back in the right direction. The only dreamers who remain are the ones who are living their own passions and dreams that come from within. They are being their true, authentic selves.

I have tried to live other people's dreams. My office job is a good example of that. I was busy working for the dream of the company, but it wasn't my dream, and I wasn't passionate about it. It's okay to say that something didn't work out because it wasn't your passion. But it's not okay to stay in a job that makes you unhappy. Take time today to tune into what makes you happy, what you are passionate about. If you could do anything in the world, what would it be? What's your dream? What do you feel would make you happy? What would you love to wake up and do every single day? Get clear on what your dream is, and work towards making it your reality.

Day 21 — Just Be

Make time to just be. What does this mean? It's letting go of everything, including your mobile phone and your to-do list. All you need to do is just be. Relax how you are, as you are.

Can you remember a time when you went anywhere without your mobile phone? We can spend so much of our time worrying about where the phone is. "Do I have my mobile on me? Is my mobile phone going flat?" Without realizing it, carrying our mobile phones creates stress because we can always be thinking, "I'd better check my mobile phone. I wonder if someone has sent me any messages? I wonder how many likes or comments I have?" It can create non-stop, mind-boggling activity, and it creates a daily practice of anxiety because we are always worrying about our mobile phones and what is going on across all the different apps and networks.

If you can't remember the last time you sat down in a chair on your own without your mobile phone, then I invite you to do so. Put your mobile on silent and out of arm's reach, perhaps in your handbag or even in a draw. Then sit on a chair or lie on the couch and get comfortable. Practice the art of relaxing and switching off, and just be. If you find that you are having a hard time sitting or lying indoors without using your mobile phone, then head for the beach and sit under a coconut tree. Listen to the waves of the ocean and immerse yourself in all of the elements of Mother Earth.

Practice the art of being. If you find that your mind wants to race off and check your e-mails, social media, or missed calls, repeat this mantra over and over again: "Just be, just be. All is safe, all is fine. Now is my time." Check in with yourself. Can you sit by yourself, as yourself, without your mobile phone? Or have you become so depend that it's now your latest addiction?

When you are constantly doing, thinking, and using your mobile phone, you are wired, and it doesn't allow you to create space within. However, when you head to the beautiful beach and take the time to admire Mother Nature as it is, it allows you to reconnect within. It will instantly bring your stress levels down and make you feel good within. Even when thoughts such as "I need to grab my mobile phone and take a photo of this, to share on social media" pop up, take a deep breath and repeat this mantra. "I just need to be, I just need to be, I just need to be." Then enjoy sitting on the beach and connecting with Mother Earth, your higher self, and the universe.

If you find yourself struggling to sit without being on your mobile phone, that's okay. Simply acknowledge the feelings and the sensations of your thoughts rising and telling you, "That's enough time of being. It's time now to pick up your mobile phone." Distract yourself by becoming mindful and looking at what is right in front of you. When you do this, you are in the present moment and are learning how to simply be instead of always feeling the need and urge to do, do, do with no let up.

Another way you can practice being is around the dinner table. Ask anyone who is joining you to try this wellness challenge of just being. Invite everyone to put their mobile phone on silent, and to simply be and enjoy each other's company. At first this might feel a little strange, especially if you are used to eating and chatting whilst looking at social media, or sharing pictures from your Instagram account, or playing funny videos and showing everyone else at the table and having your head down whilst someone is trying to talk to you from one side of the table and at the same time you are trying to eat, listen and text all at the same time. Instead of focusing on your mobile phone whilst at the table, just be.

Instead of talking about what has happened on social media, ask each other the all-important question, "How are you? Are you okay?" Get to know what is going on in each other's world.

Have a real face-to-face conversation and talk about the way you feel; be open to saying it how it is. Share what has been the most positive things to happen in your life lately, along with your own dreams and desires for this year. Have a conversation about anything and everything. Appreciate that sitting at the table with those you love is a precious time. It is a moment that can never be repeated, and after that moment, it is gone forever. That moment can never be repeated. We live in an instant world that never stops. Sadly, as human beings there comes a point in time when things do come to an end. Everything on Mother Earth in physical form is temporary, and nothing lasts forever. Unlike social media that will continue to go on, it's important when you are surrounded with those you truly love to give them your undivided love and attention. Be present.

If you start feeling anxious because you don't have your mobile phone in your hands, than repeat this mantra: "It is okay to just be. I am a human being, being."

Even though I am an online blogger, I love to just be. At first, just being mobile free was a struggle. I had become so dependent on my mobile phone, feeling like it needed to come everywhere with me. I was always on it, and checking it became addictive. It can even take over your life if you are not careful.

However, I now love practicing the art of just being. I love catching up with my family and friends without having my phone on the table. I love real life, face-to-face conversations, and socialising. I always put my phone on silent and in my bag, and when I am at the table, I never bring out my phone. I become fully present and mindful of what is going on around me. I love to be, and I love to have good, old-fashioned conversations to find out what is going on with those I truly love. We all know too well that when it comes to Facebook pages, we only ever see the happy posts and photos. I have yet to meet anyone who posts photos on Facebook of them looking mad, angry, frustrated, or crying, telling everyone how it really is. There is the real world, and then there is the online happy world.

Social media is a great way to connect with like-minded people worldwide who I normally wouldn't even know existed. I love it when I can have a one-on-one conversation with someone halfway around the world who loves the same things I do. I am still very much a social butterfly from within and love meeting people face-to-face, connecting with others socially, emotionally, and spiritually. I find this really has a human touch and a far greater effect as I get to know so much more about someone I meet in person, rather than just than looking at an online photo or profile.

Do your best to connect with other like-minded people in your local community. Take part in festivals, events, or talks so that you continue to socialise in person and not always online. Building strong face-to-face relationships can also change the way you feel. Meeting new people and making new friends can make you feel less isolated and lonely. You will be able to have a greater conversation with someone in person than you could through social media.

Making a time to be a spiritual being can be lots of fun. It gives you that sense of freedom, and it creates space within. Do your best to go mobile free and become present when you are with others. Get ready to talk, laugh, smile, and feel like you are part of something again.

YOU DID IT. YOU ARE AMAZING, AND YOU SHOULD BE PROUD

I want to say a very big thank-you for making the time to focus your attention inwards and on yourself. You did it! Twenty-one days of wellness so you can become your happiest and healthiest self. I am so proud and happy for you. Thanks for joining me and becoming your very own Spa It Girl.

Now that you learnt some of my go-to wellness tips to help you become your happiest and healthiest self, it is up to you to always choose to do things that serve your highest good and make you feel good from the inside out. It's up to you to love yourself every single day, and to always take care of yourself no matter what. I want you to live your own passion and dreams. Never give up. Always set your intentions, and know that when you make things clear on what you want and put it out there to the universe, anything and everything is possible as long as you have self-belief.

I would love for you to stay connected with me through my Spa It Girl social media channels on Instagram (@spaitgirl) and Facebook (Spa It Girl), and of course through my online blog (www.spaitgirl.com). Add the hashtag #iamaspaitgirl to share your own wellness inspiration, not to mention a photo of you rocking it with my very first self-help book, *It Starts with Me.*

Let's stay connected and continue our amazing wellness journey together. I only want the best for you, and I truly believe you deserve to feel healthy, happy, and spiritual within. Everything starts from within.

Love,
Yvette

Now that you have finished your twenty-one days of wellness, it's time to check in and see how you are truly feeling.

- How do you feel now you have finished?
- What was it like to focus on yourself for twenty-one days straight?
- What things did you do that made you feel happy?
- What things did you do that made you feel good inside?
- What did you love most about self-love Sunday?
- How will you build self-love Sunday into your life?
- What is your favourite natural skincare product to use?
- What is your favourite fruit or vegetable?
- What is your favourite way to move?
- What are three things you are now grateful for since embarking on this journey?
- How can you make time for yourself each day?
- Will you make time each day to smile?
- Will you drink green, black, or herbal tea?
- What little random acts of kindness did you find yourself doing over the last twenty-one days?
- Will you continue to do random acts of kindness to feel good?
- What was it like to close your eyes and focus inwards on your breath?

- How did focusing on your breath make you feel?
- Did you find meditating helped you with relieving stress and making you feel calmer within?
- Did you find a place, or a guided meditation teacher, that you love and can see yourself coming back to time and time again?
- What was it like to set your intentions each day?
- What was it like to set your goals daily?
- Did you find when you started focusing inwards, it helped you become more focused on your own needs, dreams, and desires?
- Did you feel that making your goals clear each day helped achieve them?
- Now that you have completed this wellness guide, do you feel that you will continue to strengthen your daily spiritual practice?
- Did you manage to get eight hours of sleep each night over the last twenty-one days?
- How did getting eight hours of beauty sleep make you feel?
- Did you find a green tea you loved drinking? Or do you still need to keep searching for one?
- Did you find that practicing mindfulness brought you into the present moment?
- What have you learnt about yourself through your wellness journey?
- Do you feel more connected and grounded within?

- Do you feel that you love yourself more from within?

- Do you feel inspired to believe in yourself more now and live your dreams?

- Can you look in the mirror and express self-love? Can you say "I love you, I love you" and mean it?

- Will you continue to practice looking in the mirror each day and strengthening your self-love practice by saying, "I love you, I love you, I really do"?

- When a negative, self-hate thought rises, will you let it fall and then focus on self-loving thoughts?

- How did it feel to just be?

- Will you continue to have social media breaks?

- Can you see yourself sitting at a table with family and friends—and without your mobile phone?

- Will you swap your manic Monday for a meditation Monday instead?

- How can you build meditation into your daily life?

- Do you feel that you are now more in touch with your inner self?

- How does it feel to change the way you feel?

- Do you believe you can live the life of your dreams?

- Do you believe in yourself?

- What is your passion?

- What is your dream?

- What makes you happy?

- What are your fears?

- What fear do you want to become bigger than?
- What fear do you feel has been holding you back for some time?
- Whom did you choose to forgive, and why?
- Whom else do you feel you need to forgive in order to release the emotional pain, anger, and hate you are holding deep inside?
- If you had to forgive yourself right here and right now, what would it be for?
- Where does your own love come from?
- Do you feel like you are a spiritual being who is now being?
- What does being a spiritual being mean to you?
- How does being a spiritual being make you feel?
- What is one thing you would love to do this year?
- What is one thing you would love to do more of?
- What is your go-to mantra?
- What is your go-to positive affirmation?
- What will you do when you are stressed? Will it be a walk, a yoga class, or catching up with a friend? What's your go-to plan?
- What is one thing you are going to try to do every day to feel good?
- If you had any advice to your younger self, what would it be? Write it down and make peace.
- If you had one wish for yourself, what would it be?

- If you had one wish for everyone else, what would it be?

Now that you have done your own self-assessment it's up to you to create the life you want and live your own dreams.

I believe you deserve to be happy, healthy, and spiritual. You should feel great from within and live a life of your own passion and dreams, not everyone else's.

Never think that anything is out of your reach, or that you can't do something. As long as you believe in yourself and practice my go-to wellness tips, anything and everything is possible. Never let others tell you that you don't have the ability to do what you truly want. Stay true to your own authentic self.

Thanks for reading my book, *It Starts with Me.* As you now know, everything starts within. The universe always has your back as long as you have your own back. You have nothing to fear, so go create and live the life you truly want. Nothing is out of your reach!

Love Yvette

ABOUT THE AUTHOR

Yvette Le Blowitz is the founder of Spa It Girl (www.spaitgirl.com), an online blog created to inspire other girls to become their happiest and healthiest selves, and to feel good within.

She is an Aussie girl on a mission, helping others to feel good within and reach their dreams through healthy spa and wellness living.

Yvette Le Blowitz was named one of Australia's leading influencers at Australia's Top Fifty Influencer Awards in 2017.

She is the it girl of the spa industry and the world's leading luxury spa travel reviewer. She is one of the world's leading spa and wellness influencers.

Yvette is a motivational speaker, a wellness coach, and a qualified and registered Fitness Australia personal trainer. She is also a Les Mills instructor.

She has been in the fitness industry for over twenty years and is a kind, loving, caring soul who loves to give more than she gets. She loves supporting R U OK Day, a charity in Australia to help raise awareness for mental illness and to break down social stigmas.

She has been a Brand Ambassador for countless of Spa, Wellness, Skincare, Hotel, Resort, Activewear, Lifestyle Brands, and she creates online content covering all aspects of the body, mind, and spirit, as well as self-help. She is a Writer, Reviewer and Contributor.

Yvette Le Blowitz is your go-to wellness it girl If you want to feel happy, healthy, and spiritual within and live your own authentic dreams.

You can stay connected with Yvette Le Blowitz at the following.

Spa It Girl: www.spaitgirl.com
Instagram: @Spaitgirl
                    @yvetteleblowitz
Face Book: Spa it Girl
YouTube: Yvette Le Blowitz
YouTube: Spa it Girl
Google+: Yvette Le Blowitz
Twitter: Spaitgirl

Be Social and Share Your Love For My Book with Your Tribe:

Hashtag:

#spaitgirl

#iamaspaitgirl

#itstartswithme

#yvetteleblowitz

Printed in the United States
By Bookmasters